EFFECTIVE TEAMBUILDING

Educated at St. Paul's School, John Adair has enjoyed a varied and colourful career. He served in the Arab Legion, worked as a deckhand on an Arctic trawler and had a spell as an orderly in a hospital operating theatre. After Cambridge he became Senior Lecturer in Military History and Leadership Training Adviser at the Royal Military Academy, Sandhurst, before becoming Director of Studies at St. George's House in Windsor Castle and then Associate Director of The Industrial Society.

In 1979 John became the world's first university Professor of Leadership Studies at the University of Surrey. He holds the degrees of Master of Arts from Cambridge University, Master of Letters from Oxford University and Doctor of Philosophy from London University, and he also is a Fellow of the Royal Historical Society.

In 2006 the People's Republic of China conferred on John the title of Honorary Professor of Leadership Studies in recognition of his 'outstanding research and contribution in the field of Leadership'. In 2009 the United Nations appointed him to be Chair of Strategic Leadership Studies at its central college in Turin.

www.ada   n

EFFECTIVE TEAMBUILDING

HOW TO MAKE A WINNING TEAM

JOHN ADAIR

PAN BOOKS

First published 1987 by Pan Books

This edition published 2015 by Pan Books
an imprint of Pan Macmillan, a division of Macmillan Publishers Limited
Pan Macmillan, 20 New Wharf Road, London N1 9RR
Basingstoke and Oxford
Associated companies throughout the world
www.panmacmillan.com

ISBN 978-1-509-81726-9

A CIP catalogue record for this book is available from
the British Library.

Typeset by SetSystems Ltd, Saffron Walden, Essex
Printed and bound by
CPI Group (UK) Ltd, Croydon, CR0 4YY

Visit www.panmacmillan.com to read more about all our books
and to buy them. You will also find features, author interviews and
news of any author events, and you can sign up for e-newsletters
so that you're always first to hear about our new releases.

CONTENTS

INTRODUCTION

'There is no strength until there is cooperation.'
Irish proverb

Few things are more satisfying in life than working in a really successful team. There are few more rewarding activities than using your qualities and skills as a leader to create such a team.

The aim of this book is to help you to choose, build, maintain and lead teams at work.

Let us start by saying that a team is a group in which the individuals share a common aim and in which the jobs and skills of each member fit in with those of the others; and let us see if we find in the course of this book that other qualities are necessary or desirable.

As any good racing driver knows, the team who designed and built the car and the team who service it before, during and after the race are as necessary for success as the person driving it. Generating effective teamwork is equally important in industry, commerce and the public services as it is in the world of professional sport, if not more so. How to get the right people in the team, how to get them to work together, how to raise their standards of performance; that in a nutshell is what this book is about.

Whether you are thinking primarily about your responsibilities as a leader or as a team member or – more likely –

with both in mind, then you should carefully work through the checklists found throughout the book. They are designed to help you to think and to apply the principles, lessons or rules of thumb to your own situation.

For this is essentially a practical book. When you have read and studied it in the light of your experience you should have most of the relevant knowledge about groups and teams that you need. Then the opportunity is yours to put it into practice.

PART ONE

UNDERSTANDING GROUPS AND INDIVIDUALS

Like any craftsman a leader must first understand their raw material. Just as a wood carver learns to work with the grain, so a leader must learn the nature of groups so that he or she can work with rather than against it.

To understand the phenomenon of groups I shall draw largely upon the tradition known as Group Dynamics. This phrase was coined by Kurt Lewin (1890–1947), a German-born psychologist and the principal figure in the early days of the Group Dynamics movement in the US during the 1940s and 1950s.

The term 'group dynamics' came to be used in two different ways. In its more general and basic sense, it was – and still is – used to describe something that is happening in all groups at all times, whether anyone is aware of it or not. Group dynamics in this general sense refers to the interacting forces within a small human group that cause it to behave the way it does.

The study by British and US social psychologists of these forces – why groups behave the way they do – was also known as Group Dynamics, which gives us the second main sense of the word. This includes the findings of such studies and the theorizing that preceded or followed observation. Group Dynamics amounted to a movement, which is why I use capital letters for it in that context.

As a training method for large numbers of leaders, the Group Dynamics approach was too time-consuming. Moreover, it was flawed by hidden assumptions of various kinds, such as those concerning leadership that I shall come to later. As a system of ideas or philosophy, the movement reflected the preoccupations of 1950s US society and especially of humanist psychologists within it. Therefore, it was much more culture-bound than its advocates were aware.

But like many ruins, Group Dynamics makes a marvellous quarry for new builders. In writing Part One I have pictured myself walking around and over the collapsed edifice of Group Dynamics and selecting here and there a stone, a length of timber, a door or piece of ironwork that I feel can still be put to use. Alternatively, I see myself as one borrowing recipes from old cookbooks and adapting them in the light of my experience. Some of the materials remain the same; others have been transformed beyond recognition. But I can think of no better foundation to effective team-building than this piecing together of an understanding of how human groups work, inspired by those remarkable pioneering efforts in Britain and the US during the last century.

1

GROUPS

*'When people are of one mind and heart,
they can move Mount Tai.'*
*Confucius (Tai was a famous mountain in Shangdou
Province – the highest known to Confucius)*

Consider a queue waiting for a bus, a cluster of people having a drink together, a crowd of angry workers on strike and a rowing eight. Which of them could be termed a group?

It is difficult to say, isn't it? For *group* is a concept. Like many concepts, such as love or friendship, it is not susceptible to a single definition. It sounds more concrete than those abstract words but it is just as hard to pin down. We all know what a group is – until we are asked!

In situations like this I usually turn to the dictionary to try and discover the picture behind the general word. The word 'group', which appears in French as *groupe* and Italian as *gruppo*, seems to be of seventeenth century German origin. It then meant: a cluster; a bunch or knot or bump; a heap; a bag (of money). This imagery suggests a number of things or people together – no more than that.

SOME DEFINITIONS CONSIDERED

The value of the word *group* largely lies in its vagueness. The biologist, for example, can use it to describe an assemblage of related organisms when he or she wishes to avoid taxonomic connotations – those that relate to classification – when the kind or degree of relationship between organisms is not clearly defined. Likewise the psychologist can employ it for a number of persons when he or she does not wish to be – or cannot be – too specific about their relation or degree of similarity. The social psychologist Edgar H. Schein, author *of Organizational Psychology* (Prentice-Hall), does not take us much further when he offers this definition:

> A psychological group is any number of people who (1) interact with one another, (2) are psychologically aware of one another, and (3) perceive themselves to be a group.

The size of the group is therefore limited by the possibilities of mutual interaction and mutual awareness. At least Schein's definition also rules out mere aggregates of people, like the crowd waiting for a train on a station platform or passengers sitting together in an airliner. Whereas work teams, committees and cliques would fall within its boundaries.

There are many variations on the themes above. Bernard M. Bass, author of *Leadership, Psychology and Organizational Behaviour* (Harper and Row), to give another instance, defined a group as:

> A collection of individuals whose existence as a collection is rewarding to the individuals (or enables them to avoid punishment). A group does not necessarily perceive itself as such. The members do not have to share common

goals. Nor are interaction, interlocking roles, and shared ways of behaviour implied in the definition, although these are common characteristics of many groups.

You will notice the points of disagreement between Schein's and Bass's definitions. Do groups perceive themselves as such? Is interaction intrinsic to them?

These examples – and disagreements – could be multiplied. They take us back to the points that *group* is a general word and that part of its attraction is that it can be used when the factors mentioned above are either not known to be present or are not clearly defined.

For precision of a language, as the Austrian philosopher Karl Popper pointed out, depends upon not burdening its terms with the task of being precise. The terms 'sand dune' and 'wind' are vague, yet for many geological purposes they are sufficiently precise. Besides, we can always qualify them, if necessary. The notion that precise knowledge requires precise definition is wrong. We operate with concepts such as 'energy' and 'light', which are not capable of being reduced to a simple definition. So it is with 'group'.

WORK GROUPS

Things are more precise if we do introduce a broad qualification and focus upon groups found in work environments – in a design office, purchasing section, night shift or executive committee. Here, for example, there is a very high probability that there will be some sort of common task. Such work groups are deep-rooted; they are part of the primary social experience for mankind. In the mists of prehistory we can imagine a group of men banding together to hunt a hairy mammoth. Perhaps some dig a pit and cover the top with branches while others locate the prey and drive it towards the trap. After the kill they divide up the meat in some order of status and take the spoils home to their cave dwellings.

It is not too fanciful to trace the descent of all working groups – expedition armies, business enterprises – from that ancestor, the primitive hunting group.

The other primary group is of course the *family*. It is instructive to consider some of the differences between work groups and families, as shown in the table below:

WORK GROUPS AND FAMILIES	
WORK GROUPS	**FAMILIES**
Have a common task – or a set of individual tasks – that tends to be explicit.	Serve two ends: companionship and the procreation and nurture of children. These are natural and often implicit.
Relationships are functional.	Relationships of parents and children are ontological.
Groups exist to work on tasks.	Families may tackle tasks – gardening together for example – but they are expressive rather than intrinsic to the family.
Leadership tends to go with competence. A young man may lead the hunting band.	Leadership traditionally tends to go with gender and seniority. Father or mother is in charge.
Work groups are often temporary.	Family implies a much greater degree of permanence.

If the *work* qualification is introduced, then many of the disagreements and differences of emphasis among psychologists about what distinguishes those collections of individuals that are groups, from those that are not, begin to fade. A collection of people is clearly a work group when it possesses most if not all of these characteristics:

- **A definable membership** – a collection of two or more people identifiable by name or type.
- **Group consciousness** – the members think of themselves as a group, have a collective perception of unity, a conscious identification with each other.
- **A sense of shared purpose** – the members have the same common task or goals or interests.
- **Interdependence** – the members need the help of one another to accomplish the purposes for which they joined the group.
- **Interaction** – the members communicate with one another, influence one another, react to one another.
- **Ability to act in a unitary manner** – the group can work as a single organism.

These factors can be pictured in a model, as below:

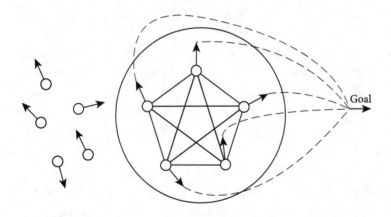

Individuals and groups

The individuals on the left hand of the diagram share no common goal. The goal arrows of the various individuals are centrifugal in this case. They lack a boundary, indicating a low consciousness of being a group and an ill-defined membership. No lines of interaction or interdependence link individuals. Clearly such a 'group' is unable to act as a whole.

Let us return to the differences between work groups and families. These differences should not be allowed to obscure the considerable overlap between them. Work groups, for example, can provide a considerable degree of mutual support and comfort. Companionship – a word directly related to *company* – is certainly experienced in organizations.

In both kinds of group, individuals acquire or shape their existing values and attitudes, beliefs and opinions, goals and ideals. The family is much more potent in this respect because a young child is more impressionable. School, which is a bridge between family and working life, comes next in potency, with the work groups we enter in young adult life, last. Traditionally, the attitudes we acquire in adult life are written in sand but the values accepted in childhood are engraved in stone. Some families, of course, are also work groups. Many of us will have watched a family of trapeze artists soaring through the air. There are family businesses that have begun with a father-son, brother-brother, sister-sister or husband-wife partnership. There have been famous family work groups, such as the celebrated Von Trapp Singers whose early story was told in *The Sound of Music* or more recently The Jackson Five.

In this context it is worth reflecting on the origins of the word *team*. The dominating image for us today is the sports team in football, baseball, hockey or cricket. But back in Anglo-Saxon times, 'team' meant 'a family' or 'offspring'. It was applied to a number of draught animals harnessed in a row because it was found that oxen or other such animals pull better together if they are related. From those teams of oxen or horses came the use of team to describe a number of persons in concerted action.

Work groups that stay together for a long time, such as an orchestra, tend to take on some of the characteristics – good or bad – of family life. Employers may regress and begin to treat their staff as children – the worst sort of paternalism or maternalism. The regiment and the business company, both institutions as well as organizations, often conceive themselves as families. As a sergeant said to a bewildered young recruit, 'I am your mother now'. A fellow officer is traditionally called a 'brother officer'. It is more than a mere analogy.

There can certainly be transfer of learning between these two fundamental kinds of group – in both directions. One study, for instance, proposed that people who find their work boring do not tend to compensate with interesting hobbies or activities in their spare time, as some sociologists – in order to defend the morality of giving people inhuman jobs and paying them well to do it – had suggested they would do. It is my belief that jobs that consist of drudgery or toil should be mechanized or automated, until we are left with an irreducible minimum of them. People should be paid exceptionally well to undertake them.

ORGANIZATIONS AND COMMUNITIES

Some psychologists distinguish between:

Primary groups	Small numbers of individuals in regular face-to-face contact
Secondary groups	Relatively large numbers – no-one has a clear picture of the other members

In working life an important instance of a larger secondary group is what we call an *organization*. It is best to think of organizations as extensions of work groups. They are larger than small groups, although at what point one shades into the other is a matter for discussion.

An organization is an association or body with an administrative and functional structure. It implies *systematic arrangement for a definite purpose*. That element of purpose is what relates it to its distant source in the hunting group and to its much nearer ancestor – the armies of the ancient world.

Institution is often used as a synonym for organization. An institution, after all, is an establishment or society *instituted* for the promotion of some object – one of a public utility, religious, charitable, educational or other nature.

To me, however, institution carries a greater overtone of permanence. We can detect here the outlines of a familiar life cycle. Many small *work groups* grow into *organizations*, which in turn become *institutions*. Not all organizations are institutions but most are.

As a rule of thumb you can define an institution by whether or not it makes provision for paying pensions – the National Health Service or UK Police Force for example. Does it have methods of selecting and releasing people – a regular inflow and outflow of individuals – while retaining its essential character and continuing purpose?

The word organization is related to the word 'organism', which reminds us that a root analogy for an organized *body* is the human body. Central to that metaphor is the concept of interdependence, that 'we are members one of another'.

From this image comes our most common metaphor for the leader – the *head* of the company, the *head* master or mistress, the *head* waiter, and so on.

By comparison *community* is more like an extension in

numbers of the family: it is a tribal or kinship grouping. It suggests a unified body of people living in a common area of land. Local communities in turn belong to the wider community of a nation or state who share both common characteristics and a number of common political, social and religious institutions that have evolved over the centuries.

I recall hearing some years back that the then chairman of one of Britain's largest nationalized industries spoke of it as a community. Is that right? Yes, because a community is any group of people with a common characteristic or interest living together within a larger society. The drawback of the word in this context is that it lies rather more in the *family* camp than in the *work group* camp. It may be better to think of such an industry as an *organization* with a definite purpose to achieve, rather than as a *community* sharing a common history and character and common interests to promote or defend.

This may seem an academic point. But the long and damaging national coal strike in Britain (1984–5) hinged on the issue of whether or not the industry was an *organization* there to produce coal at an economic rate for its customers, or a *community* itself composed of local mining communities that must at all costs be maintained, even regardless of the economic viability of the coal pits.

'Our pit was the mother of our community,' said a striking miner on television in 1985. 'The pit is dead. What happens to our community?'

The *common interest* in any work community, no matter how long it has existed, must be in giving value for money in the service or goods it provides and thereby creating satisfied customers. If that becomes impossible then the *raison d'etre* of the industry – or that particular part of it – is gone. To maximize the chances of success calls for effective and efficient working together of all concerned: in a word, teamwork.

CHECKLIST:
Yourself as a group member

- Think of the primary groups of which you are a member (work, social, family). Can you identify the needs in other group members fulfilled by their belonging to that group?

- Can you pick out some opinion, belief, value or goal that has been suggested to you, or shaped, by belonging to a group?

- What is the first small group (apart from your family) that you belonged to? What were its characteristics?

- Do you contribute best in formal work groups, such as committees, or informal groups – those created by chance or as a result of personal preference?

- What three adjectives best describe your behaviour in most groups? How, in fact, do you see yourself *now* as a group member?

- What situations within groups cause you the most problems? How do you handle them?

- What group skills would you like to develop? What strengths in behaviour in groups would you like to grow?

KEEP A DIARY

In order to write down your answers to these questions – an aid to clarity of thought – I suggest you use a stiff covered notebook. Keep it as a diary, adding ideas and insights, quotations and examples concerning teambuilding as they come to you. This book will give you some material but you should be aware while you are reading it of other sources all around you. In this way you should be able to compile your own reference book on the subject, a sourcebook of knowledge, self-understanding, inspiration – and enjoyment – for years to come.

KEY POINTS: GROUPS

- Groups of both kinds – families and work groups – together with their larger counterparts, communities and organizations, are integral to human life.
- The focus of this book is upon *work groups*. But you can apply many of its lessons in your family life or to the various social or community or religious groups to which you might belong.
- The starting point is for you to become more interested in, and more aware of, what is going on in groups. At the next group meeting you attend – preferably within two days of reading this chapter – resolve to sit and listen and observe as if you have never seen a group before in your life.
- If you are not already aware of your chief personal strengths and weaknesses as a group member, ask two or three people who know you well to give you some constructive feedback.
- Day by day you *can* become more effective in working groups. Keeping a diary of your steps in that direction over the next six months, together with key ideas from this book and elsewhere, and reviewing the contents from time to time, will help you immeasurably.

Groups are not only there to carry out tasks – they provide you with a series of unique opportunities to grow as a person.

2

SOME PROPERTIES
OF WORK GROUPS

'Even a goat and an ox must keep in step
if they are to plough together.'
Russian proverb

Work groups share certain properties with each other and
with other kinds of group. There is such a profusion of them
that the quest for similarities may seem a vain one. But it is
possible to identify characteristics that all groups possess,
albeit in varying degrees. These properties have received
much attention from researchers. They are of course overlapping and interactive, so it is better to regard them as facets
of a single diamond than as separate entities.

In this chapter I shall outline a set of these properties. The
list of them below is by no means exhaustive. Some of the
properties, such as *common task*, *roles* and *leadership*, are
reserved for later chapters but they cannot be divorced from
the factors described in this chapter.

BACKGROUND

Each group has a historical background, or lack of it, which influences the way it behaves.

The members of a new group assembling for the first time may have to devote much of their initial energy to getting acquainted with one another and deciding what needs to be done and how to do it. A well-established group, on the other hand, will be better acquainted with the situation. They may be assumed to know what to expect from each other and how to define the group's task. Ways of working together will have evolved. But such a group may also have developed habits that impair its effectiveness, such as unpunctuality, poor listening or wasting time.

Members come to a meeting of a new group or team with some expectations. They may have a clear idea of what it is about or they may be uncertain about what is going to happen. They may be looking forward to being in that group or dreading it; they may feel deeply concerned or indifferent. In some cases the boundaries around the group's freedom of action may be tightly drawn by its terms of reference, or so poorly defined that the group doesn't know what its boundaries or limits are.

The history of the group in terms of its past successes and failures – its record in pursuing common objectives – is a central ingredient in background, relating as it does to group morale. Whether or not membership of the group in the past has been satisfying to each member is also another ingredient. The sense of sharing a common history – people, places and events – tends to bind people together. It gives them a dimension, a reference point, a depth, a quarry for memories and, often, a source of inspiration.

Most groups, especially those having relatively long histories, develop ceremonies and rituals to help them deal with certain events. These include birthday celebrations, 'farewell drinks' when a member leaves the group, and 'initiation rites' of various kinds.

A crucial factor in group or team formation is therefore the amount of time that has been spent together. It takes time for a group personality to take shape. Nature does not work quickly. Relationships are as tender as plants when young but as strong as oaks when formed. If you want to build a team it is essential that you do get it together – and hold it together – over a significant period of time.

CHECKLIST:
Group background

- What is the group's story? When did it come into being and for what purpose?

- Has the purpose of the group changed? If so, when did this occur and why?

- What is the composition of the group? What is the previous experience and personal history of each member? How were they related?

- What are the key experiences of success and failure that the group shares?

- What are the expectations of each member about the group and their role in it?

PARTICIPATION PATTERN

In the snapshot of any given moment a particular partici-pation pattern can be observed in every group. For example, it may be all *one-way* traffic, with the leader or some other member conducting a monologue; or it may be *two-way*, with the leader talking to members and members responding to him or her; or it may be *multi-directional*, with all members talking to one another and to the group as a whole.

In any given group you may notice that one of these patterns tends to be prevalent over a period of time. In other groups there may be a considerable variation within quite short spaces.

There is no reason to believe that any one pattern of participation is always best: it depends upon the situation. But many studies point to the common sense conclusion that the more that members participate, the more that they will tend to be involved in the group.

It should not be assumed, of course, that silent members are necessarily uninterested. These members may be simply thinking. As leader, you should ask yourself the following questions about them. Are they really interested? What prevents them from speaking? It may be that they want to speak but never have the opportunity to join in the discussion because someone (is it you?) is talking overmuch. If so, you should practise the skill of *gatekeeping*: 'Malcolm, we have heard your views at some length but Sally hasn't said anything for the last hour, though doubtless she has

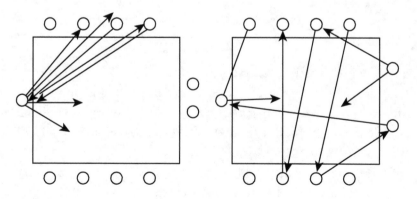

Participation patterns

been thinking a lot. Sally, have you anything to contribute to next year's objectives on the marketing front ... No, Malcolm you can't just clarify your last point (laughter) – Sally?'

It is very easy, and often useful in teambuilding, to chart the participation pattern during a defined period of discussion, thus providing some objective data about this aspect of group working, as in the diagram on the previous page.

CHECKLIST:
Participation patterns

- How much of the talking is done by the leader, how much is done by the other members?

- To who are questions usually addressed – the group as a whole, the leader, or particular members?

- Do the members who don't talk much appear to be interested and listening alertly (non-verbal participation), or do they seem bored and apathetic?

- Do the leader and other senior members in the group practise *gatekeeping* skills – to open the door for lower status members to talk?

COMMUNICATION

How well do group members understand each other's meanings: how clearly are they communicating their ideas, values and feelings? If some members are using a highly specialized technical vocabulary they may be talking over the heads of the rest of the group.

Sometimes a group will develop a specialized vocabulary of its own, a kind of verbal shorthand, or private jokes that aren't understood by new members or outsiders. This can facilitate communication within the group but can create problems within the organization as a whole.

Communication in a group will be greatly enhanced if each member is skilled in speaking, listening, writing and reading. In fact a person tends to be stronger in one or two of these activities than the others, giving him a profile of strengths and weaknesses as a communicator. In my companion book *Effective Communication* you can read more about the Five Principles of Good Speaking (and good communication as a whole). They are: Be Clear, Be Prepared, Be Simple, Be Vivid and Be Natural.

The good listener is one who looks upon listening as a positive, searching, active and cooperative activity. Too often when a person is not speaking at a meeting, he or she spends their time framing their intervention: they *hear* what is being said but do not *listen* in a way that grasps the core meaning of someone else's contribution, enabling them to elucidate it if necessary and build upon it or weave it into the discussion.

Even non-verbal communication can often be eloquent. A person's posture, facial expression and gestures tell a great deal about what he or she is thinking and feeling. The member who pulls his chair, for example, away from the table and gazes out of the window is saying something to you and the rest of the group.

CHECKLIST:
Communication in a group

- Are members expressing their ideas clearly, simply and concisely?

- Are visual aids and other tools of communication used in a way that suggests thorough preparation by members?

> **CHECKLIST:**
> **Communication in a group (*Cont.*)**
>
> * Do any general concepts, such as 'maximum profit' or 'customer service' get sufficiently defined so that the group agrees on their meaning?
> * Do members often adopt contributions previously made and build their ideas on to them?
> * Do members feel free to ask for clarification when they don't understand a statement?
> * Are responses to statements frequently irrelevant?

COHESIVENESS

The cohesiveness of a group is determined by the strength of the bonds that bind the individual parts together into a unified whole. This property is related to other more traditional concepts such as morale and team spirit. Cohesiveness, the strength of attraction of the group for its members, is also linked to the degree of interest commitment to the common task. It is sometimes referred to as the 'we-feeling' of a group – the extent to which members talk in terms of 'we' and 'us'. Symptoms of low cohesion include the absence of such words from the group's vocabulary.

Many studies have identified the conditions under which groups tend to become more cohesive. The more important factors are:

Physical proximity   People working together in the same place will tend to form a group, even if their work is not interdependent. Length of time together increases the tendency towards cohesiveness.

Same or similar work	People doing identical or similar work are faced with the same problems and can help each other in various ways – a source of group formation.
Homogeneity	Cohesiveness in groups tends to be greater if members share such characteristics as race, age, sex, social status and attitudes or values.
Personality	Members do not have to be alike in personality, but some combinations of personality work better than others – where social needs are strong and there are not too many over-dominant or disruptive people.
Communication	Cohesiveness will be greater if members can communicate easily with others, and less if distance, noise or organizational arrangements make communication difficult.
Size	It becomes more difficult for groups of more than twelve or fifteen members to develop group cohesion. Small groups are much more likely to do so.

Cohesiveness is enhanced if belonging to it is *rewarding* to individuals in several ways. Studies have confirmed that members are most likely to be attracted to a group if it has a successful record in competition with other groups. High pay and prestige and the consequences of belonging to such successful groups are also incentives for wanting to become or remain a member.

Methods of pay or working conditions can foster or retard the development of group cohesiveness in industry. A group bonus scheme, rather than individual incentive schemes, emphasizes the shared nature of the common task. The efforts of each member of the assembly line or research group will then serve the interests of all the others. But strong group pressures may then build upon slow workers who are holding back the team. Such a 'passenger' may be forced out of the group.

Group cohesiveness is a double-edged weapon. The table below lists the pros and cons of the cohesive group:

THE COHESIVE GROUP	
ADVANTAGES	**DISADVANTAGES**
Greater cooperation	Low tolerance of 'slackers'
More/easier communication	Life more difficult for new entrants
Increased resistance to frustration	
	Restricts entry for new ideas
Reduced labour turnover	Resists changes in work practices
Lower absenteeism	Seen as awkward/combative by other groups, thus reducing intergroup cooperation

A leader should always be on the alert for the unwanted side effects of group cohesiveness. Thus, one of a leader's jobs is to protect individuals against the power of the group. Group power can sometimes be exercised unfairly on individuals for a variety of reasons. Groups can make an individual into a scapegoat, for example, as if tacitly agreeing to make him or her responsible for the whole burden of corporate failure. The psychology of this act, probably largely unconscious, is quite different from the proper doctrine of individual accountability, a dimension that should not be cancelled by group membership.

Any form of such victimization should be stopped by the leader if for no other reason than that it will eventually destroy the group's unity.

The essentials of morale

'Morale is a state of mind. It is that intangible force which will move a whole group of men to give their last ounce to achieve something, without counting the cost to themselves; that makes them feel they are part of something greater than themselves. If they are to feel that, their morale must, if it is to endure – and the essence of morale is that it should endure – have certain foundations. These foundations are spiritual, intellectual and material, and that is their order of importance. Spiritual first, because only spiritual foundations can stand real strain. Next intellectual, because men are swayed by reason as well as feeling. Material last – important, but last – because the very highest kinds of morale are often met when material conditions are lowest.'

Field Marshal Lord Slim in *Defeat into Victory* (1956)

Group cohesiveness is not the same as morale although they are like cousins. *Morale* was a word introduced in the last century to describe a group's or individual's *condition* in relation to confidence, discipline and sense of common purpose. It covers the condition of people's attitudes to the task, their loyalty to one another and their self-respect. The links of morale with *esprit de corps* and group cohesiveness are obvious. When morale is high we carry out work in the face of danger or difficulty. When it is low we are more vulnerable to criticism, hardship and failure.

CHECKLIST:
Cohesiveness in a group

- How well is the group working together as a unit?

- What sub-groups or 'lone wolves' are there and how do they affect the group?

- What evidence is there of interest or lack of interest on the part of members of the group (or groups in the organization) in what is happening in the area of the common task?

- Do members speak to the leader of 'your group' or 'our group?

- Despite reverses is the level of confidence high? Is there still a strong sense of purpose and resolve?

- Is the team spirit in evidence? Do members mutually support and encourage each other as well as working well together in a technical sense?

ATMOSPHERE

Although atmosphere, like morale, is an intangible thing, it is usually fairly easy to sense. It is often referred to as the 'social climate' of the group, with such characteristics as 'warm, friendly, relaxed, informal or free' in contrast to 'cold, hostile, tense, formal or restrained'. Atmosphere affects how members feel about a group and the degree of spontaneity in their participation. Atmosphere may be temporary; climate implies a prevailing condition.

'Teams generate a climate of loyalty', writes Tom Douglas, author of *Groups* (Tavistock), 'which stems from the acceptance of dependence on others to achieve a desired outcome. There is something of the secret society about all successful teams. Members accept the skills and knowledge of other members as a common resource and the sense of sharing and shared experience, which distinguishes members from non-members, is high.'

Atmosphere or climate relates to morale, which is an atmospheric word if ever there was one.

What is the difference between atmosphere and morale? *Atmosphere* is usually fairly easy to sense: you feel it yourself. On the other hand *morale* is inferred from observations of behaviour and it is an inference about the state of people observed. It is a vital part of leadership to build up the right atmosphere or climate and to change if it is wrong. Let me quote some sentences from N. Hamilton's *Monty: The Making of a General* (Hamish Hamilton), citing Field Marshal Montgomery's speech to his staff when he took over the Eighth Army before the Battle of El Alamein in 1942:

> You do not know me, I do not know you, but we have got to work together. Therefore, we must understand each other, we must have confidence in each other. I have only been here a few hours, but from what I have seen and heard since I arrived, I am prepared to say here and now that I have confidence in you. We will work together as a team. I believe that one of the first duties is to create what I call atmosphere. I do not like the general atmosphere I find here – it is an atmosphere of doubt, of looking back. All that must cease. I want to impress upon everyone that the bad times are over and it will be done. If anybody here thinks it cannot be done, let him go at once. I do not want any doubters. It can be done and it will be done beyond any possibility of doubt.

Morale

Morale
Shows itself
As a state of mind
Radiating confidence
In people

Where each member
Feels sure of his own niche,
Stands on his own abilities
And works out his own solutions
– Knowing he is
Part of a team

Where no person
Feels anxiety or fear
Or pressure to be better
Than someone else

Where there exists
A sharing of ideas
A freedom to plan
A sureness of worth,
And a knowledge
That help is available
For the asking

To the end that
People grow and mature
Warmed by a friendly climate

Anon

The verses opposite describe some valuable inward features of a work group, but they do not touch the way in which it responds to outer events. The latter is also a vital dimension of morale.

Mark Twain once said: 'Everyone talks about the weather but no one does anything about it'. You can affect the climate in your organization by what you are, what you do, and what you say.

CHECKLIST:
Group atmosphere and morale

- Would you describe your primary work group as warm or cool, friendly or hostile, relaxed or tense, informal or formal, free or restrained?

- Can opposing views or negative feelings be expressed without fear of retribution?

- Is morale in the group low? Is there an 'atmosphere of doubt, of looking back'?

STANDARDS

Every group, if it is together for some time, develops a code of conduct or set of *standards* about what is proper and acceptable behaviour. These include such subjects as what matters may be discussed; what is taboo (such as religion or politics); how well members listen to each other's opinions; how far it is proper to volunteer one's services; the length and intensity of work that's considered right and fair; whether or not pilfering is permissible; and many more 'do's and don'ts'.

It may be difficult for a new member to identify and adopt a group's standards if they differ from those of other groups he or she has experienced, for these standards are usually implicit rather than written down. Indeed, at a given time, a group might be confused about what its own standards actually are.

A *group-norm* – an oft-used phrase in the textbooks – is simply an authoritative standard. The word 'norm' originated in the nineteenth century and derives from the Latin word *norma* meaning a builder's or carpenter's square, the tool that gave him the perfect right angle.

Over-conformity to accepted norms can stultify growth and inhibit creativity. For creative individuals will always tend to deviate from or transcend the established ways of doing things or thinking about the world in which the group is set. Therefore norms can be battle lines between groups and individuals. This tension is the theme of a later chapter.

Standards can be broken down into different families, which to some extent function differently:

Work	These concern the best and easiest methods of working, and usually include some unwritten folklore: how fast, how hard, how long, to what standard, how safety-minded and so on. Professional training seeks to inculcate certain standards of conduct so that individuals follow them whatever the social pressures or when they are working on their own.
Attitudes	Attitudes, beliefs and values tend to be shared in groups. The fact that a group accepts a common attitude does not of course mean it is necessarily true. Groups may also share a common interpretation of the past, often coloured by some collective myths!

Interpersonal behaviour	There are norms about what can be discussed and what cannot, whether or not it is right to interrupt, where to go for lunch and so on. Such tacit agreements to proceed socially in a standard way help to make the behaviour of others predictable, orderly and satisfying. Shared routines can be enjoyed. Norms keep interpersonal conflicts to the minimum; they avoid conflicts over such potential problems as helping, allocation of jobs and division of rewards.
Clothes and language	Members of a group often resemble each other in their dress and physical appearance. They often use a private language of their own: slang, technical terms related to the job, nicknames for people and places, subcultural vocabularies, such as obscenities. Especially prevalent in what have vividly been called 'ball and chain groups'.
Moral standards	These range from the permissible limits of timewasting, scrounging, cheating on incentive schemes to norms concerning ethical practice, truth-telling and sexual behaviour.

Standards begin life as a rough-and-ready form of consensus among the original members of the group as to what will work for them if they are to attain their goals and hold together in unity. Some members – the leader or leading members – have more influence over this process than others. These latter, less influential members, together with all new recruits to the group, are expected to adopt these norms. Several factors are at work to help them to do so.

In the first instance, people falling short of a norm or consciously choosing to deviate from it become the target for a great deal of persuasion and friendly pressure to conform from the majority. They can conform or leave the group. If they continue to stand out they risk punishment. There is a Japanese proverb, still much quoted today in Japan, which says that the nail that sticks up is going to get knocked on the head.

The mildest form of punishment is group displeasure. As that escalates the treatment of deviants becomes more severe. When in difficulties they receive no help; they are given the worst jobs; their work is interfered with. They may be rejected, given the silent treatment or 'sent to Coventry' as the English phrase goes, or even physically attacked. It is as if the group has reserves of the milk of human kindness; once these have been exhausted it can turn nasty.

It is impossible to avoid the moral issue here. First you have to decide if the norm being urged is good or bad. Then you have to decide whether or not the form of group pressure being applied is justifiable or not in the circumstances.

In normal situations we do not have to make these judgements solely on our own or from scratch. Society has a tradition of social and moral norms, the minimum standards among them being enshrined in constitutions and laws. The law does also rule out many of the obvious abuses of group power over deviant individuals. You can reason with a strike-breaking colleague; you cannot – or rather should not – break his or her arm.

CHECKLIST:
Group standards

- Can you identify any unwritten standards in the group?
- Are there marked deviations from these standards by one or more members?
- Do these standards seem to be well understood by all members, or is there confusion about them?
- Which of the group's standards seem to help and which seem to hinder the group's progress?

STRUCTURE AND ORGANIZATION

Groups have both a formal and an informal organizational structure. The formal structure, which might be highly visible (officers, committees, appointed positions), represents the division of labour among members so that essential functions are performed. Beyond formal structure there is also informal, much of which comes into play behind the scenes. It concerns how things actually get done according to the relative prestige, influence, power, seniority and persuasiveness of members.

The concept of roles, discussed in the next chapter, is related to structure. Structure can almost be defined as a *hierarchy* of roles within the group or organization.

Structure in work groups ought to be directly related to the common task. In so far as the needs of the task are changing, so structure should be flexible or malleable to alteration. Ideally there should not be a dichotomy or chasm between the formal and informal structures. Although all organizations should encourage communication outside 'proper channels', the better designed they are the less chance should there be that they are run on some secret 'old boy net'.

> **CHECKLIST:**
> **Group structure and organization**
>
> - What kind of formal structure or organization is there within the group?
> - What is the invisible structure: who really controls and who defers to others?
> - Is the structure understood and accepted by the members?
> - Is the structure appropriate to the group's purpose and tasks?

GROUPS IN MOTION

So far we have been looking at some of the key elements or variables that make up a group – its properties or dimensions – from an analytical point of view. But groups are alive; they do not stand still in time and space. The analytical approach needs to be complemented by a holistic view of the moving, living, dynamic whole.

Not only is the group moving as a unit but the various elements within it are constantly interacting. A change in procedure will affect the atmosphere, which will affect the participation pattern, which will affect cohesion, which will affect morale and so on.

Various attempts have been made to discern phases or patterns within the constant flux of group life.

Many theorists in the Group Dynamics movement, for example, made analogies describing the process of group formation as a spiral, a series of cycles, or a series of stages that succeed each other as growth occurs.

Groups would work on a problem, and then as if by agreement withdraw from it, only to return to the same ground some time later but upon a higher plane. Knowledge of this spiralling effect was useful not least because it helped me as a teacher to time my interventions. For instance, it was worth waiting for the 'upward thermals' before making comments. Remarks made when the group was not in a work phase or cycle, but 'resting' or withdrawing, were not as likely to be effective.

Consistent and identifiable stages of development in all groups probably do not exist. Group growth is a gradual process in which themes and subtleness may intertwine but in which the dramatic quality is the wholeness. The closest analogy to my mind is a musical symphony, with tunes, phrases and moods interwoven into a moving pattern.

Any breakdown into phases by a process of analysis therefore runs the double danger of over-simplifying and also destroying that very holistic quality that constitutes the group. Analysis leads to abstraction, which in turn leads us away from the concrete, unique, whole group with whom you may be working in your daily life.

There are probably no clear and finite *stages* of development. But that does not mean there are no consistent sequential changes. Not every teenager goes through a stage of moodiness but there are changes in such a period of life that tend to be accompanied by moodiness. Not every mother feels post-natal depression but there is a tendency for that to happen.

This is the nearest we can get to regularity. It does appear that in some groups change takes a cyclic or spiral form, with movement backwards and forwards. In other groups change seems to happen in sudden leaps and bounds, interspersed with plateau periods where no change occurs. In other groups there are regressive movements as well as dramatic and unpredictable spurts. Again you may be able to think of analogies in the development of individuals you know well – or indeed in your own life history. You should bear these factors in mind when considering the group development model in the table overleaf.

GROUP DEVELOPMENT		
	GROUP STRUCTURE	**TASK ACTIVITY**
Forming	Considerable anxiety, testing to discover the nature of the situation, what help can be expected from leader or convener and what behaviour will or will not be appropriate.	What is the task? Members seek the answers to that basic question, together with knowledge of the rules and the methods to be employed.
Storming	Conflict emerges between sub-groups; the authority and/or competence of the leader is challenged. Opinions polarize. Individuals react against efforts of the leader or group to control them.	The value and feasibility of the task is questioned. People react emotionally against its demands.
Norming	The group begins to harmonize; it experiences group cohesion or unity for the first time. Norms emerge as those in conflict are reconciled and resistance is overcome. Mutual support develops.	Cooperation on the task begins; plans are made and work standards laid down. Communication of views and feelings develop.
Performing	The group structures itself or accepts a structure that fits most appropriately its common task. Roles are seen in terms functional to the task and flexibility between them develops.	Constructive work on the task surges ahead; progress is experienced as more of the group's energy is applied to being effective in the area of their common task.

These phrases are fairly recognizable to any normally perceptive person with experience in work groups. Where there is an unresolved problem, of who is in charge for example, a power struggle may develop among members who desire to have things move their way or who may enjoy controlling others or power for its own sake. Such people in such unresolved control situations will tend to engage in various persuasive methods of controlling others, such as advice giving, argument or confrontation. Strategies for manipulating others may be resorted to, possibly in sub-groups outside the total group. People may appeal in vain to the appointed or elected leader to check this competition for power. Others may argue against all forms of control, as if enjoying the apparent freedom in the lack of any organization.

The resolution of this phase, and the eventual emergence of the group into the stage of *performance*, is not the end of the story. The group that is already a team in ore may go on to become the refined metal of a high performance team. The processes by which high tempered steel can be refined and wrought from the full ore of average performance are the theme of Part Two.

The group may equally lapse into decline, known as the *dorming* phase. Here, group structure becomes governed by routine and systems – everything has to go through 'proper channels' and the group spirit becomes ossified into a comfortable and cosy togetherness. Task activity falls off in quantity and quality, but the group does not really mind ... it is so tired ... yawn, yawn. It is so satisfied by past achievements that it is content to leave the unconquered peaks to the young thrusting groups coming into being all around it.

Not all groups behave in this way. Some complete their job and disperse. Some complete a job and say 'that was enjoyable – can we find something else to do.'

KEY POINTS: SOME PROPERTIES OF
WORK GROUPS

- Groups share a number of properties that can to some extent be abstracted and discussed in general. They include a common background or history (or lack of it), participation patterns, communication, cohesiveness, atmosphere, standards, structure and organization.
- Groups change and grow because they exist in time as well as space. Seek to understand the processes at work within them as they move forwards by fits and starts, progressing and regressing. Then you will be in a better position to intervene helpfully.
- Four simple stages – forming, storming, norming and performing – will serve you as a good introduction to the story, especially if you are present at the birth of a new group.
- Group cohesiveness is essential – but remember that it brings some potential disadvantages in its train. As a leader you must always watch out for these danger signs and then take action to counter them.
- Watch out, too, for the group norms. Are they as you would want them to be? If not, change them by your words and examples.

To lead is to serve, nothing more and nothing less.

3

ROLES

'We have to consider our responsibilities, not ourselves. We are to regard the duties of which we are capable, but not our capabilities simply considered. There is to be no complacent self-contemplation. When the self is viewed, it must always be in the most intimate connection with its purposes.'
William Gladstone, former UK Prime Minister

A role is a capacity in which someone acts in relation to others. It is a metaphor from the theatre, where a role is a part assumed by one actor in a play while others are assuming other parts.

This origin gives the word some persistent undertones. A dramatic role is acted or played; it is taken on temporarily and dropped at the end of the play.

But having a role in real life need not connote 'play-acting' or temporariness. Rightly understood, the concept can illuminate behaviour in work groups, families and society.

VARIETIES OF ROLE

Role tends to be a favourite word among sociologists. But in my opinion to apply it to all social relations, however transitory or spontaneous, is to water down the concept to the point where it becomes vacuous and useless.

A role in the untheatrical sense, in the context of work groups and families, organizations and communities, should usually be reserved for those relationships that are sufficiently structured to have a common name, such as teacher–pupil, leader–follower, doctor–patient, husband–wife. Role behaviour is the way of acting that is considered appropriate to a role. Various factors – functional, traditional or custom – shape what is thought to be this appropriate behaviour.

An important insight from social studies is that the 'occupant' of a role is to some degree the recipient of *expectations* from others as to what behaviour is appropriate to his or her role. If a policeman stops your car in heavy traffic in order to tell you a joke you may be justifiably apprehensive: he has stepped outside his role. You do not *expect* him to behave like that.

The concept of role, then, can be applied to life. Indeed the Greeks had a proverb: 'Life is a stage, so learn to play your part.' Shakespeare's words echo that thought:

> All the world's a stage
> And all the men and women merely players:
> They have their exits and their entrances;
> And one man in his time plays many parts,
> His acts being seven ages. At first the infant,
> Mewling and puking in the nurse's arms.
> And then . . .

In these oft-quoted lines from *As You Like It,* Shakespeare goes on to list the seven ages of a man's life. He then characterizes three of them by the roles in a contemporary drama that the youth and mature man might play during these seven ages: lover, soldier and magistrate.

Real life is inevitably more complex but the rough division of roles between family life and work in Shakespeare's list is perpetuated on this wider front. Our roles, of course, change suddenly or subtly as we move through Shakespeare's seven ages of man. Here are some examples:

Family roles	*Work roles*
Son or daughter	Team leader
Husband or wife	Shop steward
Father or mother	Senior trades union official
Grandfather or mother	Manager
Aunt or uncle	Executive director
Brother or sister	Chief executive officer
	Chairman

We can distinguish between the more *formal* roles such as being a judge, and the more *informal* ones such as lover and friend. The latter are found more in the sphere of personal relationships. In working groups, you should note here that the role of leader is sometimes formal (for example, the appointed Squadron Leader of a fighter squadron or CEO of a company) and sometimes more informal, the leader who emerges naturally from the group and has no official position.

Roles are also connected with *status* or social position in work groups or organizations. As we have seen, as part of group structuring, different individuals will occupy different roles. Low status members at meetings will be recognizable because they will not talk much, be polite, deferential and generally have little notice taken of them.

Thus some form of *hierarchy* or 'pecking order' emerges in all groups. Financial reward, rank and status often go together but not by any means always. Sometimes status (as in the British honours system) is divorced from financial reward.

In working groups the role that naturally carries the highest status is that of the leader. He or she heads the hierarchy, implicit or explicit, within the group. To this key role we must now turn.

THE ROLE OF LEADER

It is now widely accepted that the most important role in a small work group is that of the leader. We should attempt to distinguish here, as always, between the *role* and the *person* performing the role. A role can be seen in general and impersonal terms. We can shape our notion of a role by looking objectively at the situation, at the rights and obligations involved, and above all at the requirements of the task to be done. Some roles, however, are likely to call for certain personal qualities. Leadership is clearly in this category. Every individual leader who fulfils the leadership role will therefore do so in his or her own unique style, governed by the unique combination of traits – personality and character – he or she brings to the role.

Despite these personal differences I have argued that the core role of all leaders is the same. The role is to help the group to achieve its common task, to maintain it as a unity and to ensure that each individual contributes his or her best.

That definition, to repeat the point, applies to leaders in all working situations, at any level of structure in their role relationships, whether they are formal or informal, elected or appointed, imposed or emergent.

This view of the leadership role differed from that taught in the Group Dynamics movement. There the leadership role as such was certainly not emphasized. 'Most groups do have appointed leaders', conceded Matthew B. Miles, an influential figure in the movement, 'as a kind of 'safety net' or guarantee that *someone* will fill needed functions but the approach taken here assumes that the appointed leader and members alike may exert leadership'.

This underestimate of the role of leadership in the Group Dynamics movement, noted critically by early commentators and repaired later in the work of some social psychologists, stemmed from unique situational factors in the American culture at the time.

ROLE CONFLICT

Role conflict exists at work as well. Whatever the job titles, managers occupy three roles. The first role of *leader* is so preoccupying that the other two roles of *follower or subordinate* and *colleague* are often overlooked. The latter two roles are more shadowy. But there can be considerable tensions between your obligations to the group working for you and your loyalty to your superior or your cooperation with colleagues of the same status as yourself in other parts of the organization. Each man is a trinity of three persons.

Role conflict in that sense does not exhaust the stress problems related to work roles, as the 'Role problems' chart on page 43 illustrates.

Lack of clarity and comfort in your role can cause insecurity, lack of confidence, irritation, anxiety and even anger among those around you. All these add up to unwelcome stress. As we all know, a challenge can be invigorating. But it can easily degenerate into a form of stress that is, by definition, damaging. There is a world of difference between working under pressure and working under strain. The symptoms of such *role strain* are:

Stress	Often accompanied by physical symptoms. Behaviour characterized by: irritability, scrupulous concern for trivial detail; emphasis on precision; a tendency to dichotomize things into 'black' or 'white'; resort to stereotyped responses; increased sensitivity to group pressures and organizational rumours.
Low morale	Often expressed as: dissatisfaction with the job; cynical comments about the organization; low confidence in colleagues and team members; a sense of futility.
Communication difficulties	Often the person becomes preoccupied, silent and withdrawn. He or she is hard to talk to.

These symptoms, of course, may be associated with stress arising from sources other than role strain. If the underlying problem is to do with roles, then action should be taken as suggested in the table of 'Role problems' opposite.

KEY POINTS: ROLES

- Just as we buy our clothes ready-made 'off the peg' so most of the roles we occupy or aspire to at work exist in their own right. A team can be thought of as a structure of jobs.
- If a relationship moves into action then roles will begin to emerge. Conversely, if you start with a role, it will tell you what actions and relationships are expected from you.

ROLE PROBLEMS		
PROBLEM	**CAUSES**	**STRATEGIES**
Role overload	Not the same as work overload. It comes when a person has too many roles for him or her to handle at a time. It is the variety rather than the quantity of work that is experienced here as confusing and tiring.	Downgrade the priority level of some roles, accepting from self a lower performance level. Agree a reassignment of role responsibilities.
Role underload	This occurs characteristically when an individual is given a role that falls far short of his or her self-concept. Whether it is or not is irrelevant: it is the individual's perception that causes role underload.	Take on someone else's role in addition to your own. Use your imagination to develop the role.
Role ambiguity	Arises when there is uncertainty in the mind of the focal person or members of his or her group, colleagues or superiors as to precisely what his or her role is at any given time. Ambiguity is not necessarily a bad thing; it can aid creativity. But uncertainty can be experienced as unhelpful and stressful.	Ask for clarification from key members of the organization with a stake in the problem. Negotiate with them a clearer concept of your role.

- Roles should never be completely defined even if it is possible to do so – that would leave no room for your creativity as a person. But you should strive to be as clear as possible about any given role.
- Many people have impoverished concepts of the roles they occupy. Draw upon as many sources as you can to enlarge and deepen your understanding of these roles.
- This applies especially to the three basic roles at work – *leader, subordinate* and *colleague.*

Role without personality is empty but personality without role is ineffective.

4

MEMBER FUNCTIONS

Together
Everyone
Achieves
More

Perhaps the most enduring contribution of the study of group dynamics to our understanding of groups is the distinction between *task* and *maintenance* behaviour. Task behaviour is self-explanatory. In this context, maintenance means holding the group together or maintaining it as a unity.

This discovery of two distinct areas of concern and response in groups was a real milestone. The ways in which people responded could be categorized in terms of *functions* – what you *do* or *say* rather than what you *are* as a person. Much previous talk about functions in organizations could now be earthed in the empirically discovered realities of group life: *the need to achieve the common task and the need to be held together as a working entity.*

There was another important distinction concerning group work made in Group Dynamics: this time *content* and *process*. The content is what the group is talking about, while process concerns such issues as how it makes decisions. Everyone knows what a process is but it is still very difficult to define it. The application of heat to uncooked food is the 'process' of cooking: it changes materials from one form to another.

There is a potential confusion here because the contrast cannot be equated with that between task and maintenance. They are different sets of ideas.

TASK AND GROUP MAINTENANCE FUNCTIONS

In Chapter 2 we looked at what happens in the early life of a group. It must be reiterated that the groups that formed the subject of these studies were training groups in the Group Dynamics movement. Consequently they were rather peculiar if not unique.

The impact of situational influences was not so readily understood then as now. Therefore hesitation is called for before transferring lessons to work group settings that may be familiar to you in real life. Nevertheless, I hold that the Group Dynamics movement did throw up some valuable insights relevant to all who work with groups, insights that we would be foolish to let slip into obscurity.

It is especially important to bear this provenance in mind when reading the next few pages on functions. They are based on the work of two group theorists, Kenneth D. Benne and Paul Sheats in 1948, as cited in their *Journalism of Social Issues* article 'Functional Roles of Group Members'. Their lists of functions clearly relate to the unstructured discussion group-type situation. Indeed, Benne and Sheats developed their lists of functions for the First National Training Laboratory in Group Development, held in the US in 1947. The lists followed closely the analysis of participation functions as used in coding the content and process of group discussions for their research purposes.

You will notice that the authors talk about member *roles* rather than *functions*. To personalize functions like that strikes me as wrong, a point I shall return to later. For my part I prefer to keep the word *role* for relationships with some more marked degree of structure, ones with a pattern of conduct associated with them – recognized in breach as well as in observance. I should emphasize again that if any form of social relation, however transitory or spontaneous, came to be regarded as a role relation, the concept will become so general and all-embracing as to lose its value as a tool of social analysis. However, I have felt it right here to reproduce the categories exactly in the way that Benne and Sheats wrote them.

GROUP TASK ROLES

Benne and Sheats assumed that they were dealing with discussion groups whose task was roughly to select, define and solve common problems. The roles they identified relate to functions of facilitating and coordinating these group problem-solving activities. The inappropriateness of their use of the word 'role' is underlined when they go on to say that 'each member may of course enact more than one role in any given unit of participation and a wide range of roles in successive participations'. Here are their twelve categories:

Initiator-contributor	Suggests to group new ideas, new group goals, or new definition of problem; proposes new procedures, ways of handling some difficulty or forms of organization.
Information seeker	Asks for clarification of suggestions in terms of factual accuracy; seeks information and facts relevant to problem.

Opinion seeker	Asks not for facts but for clarification of the values pertinent to what the group is undertaking or involved in the various suggestions.
Information giver	Offers facts or generalizations that are 'authoritative' or relates his or her own experience to the group problem.
Opinion giver	States his or her belief or opinion pertinently to a suggestion made or alternatives being canvassed.
Elaborator	Spells out suggestions in terms of examples or developed meanings; offers reasons for suggestions and tries to deduce consequences of following them.
Coordinator	Shows or clarifies the relationships among various ideas and suggestions and tries to pull them together; attempts to coordinate the activities of members or sub-group.
Orienter	Defines the position of the group with respect to its goals; summarizes what has happened; points to departures from agreed directions; raises questions upon direction that the group discussion is taking.
Evaluator-critic	Subjects the accomplishment of the group to some standard or set of standards.
Energizer	Prods the group to action or decision; attempts to stimulate or arouse the group to 'greater' or 'higher quality' activity.
Procedural technician	Expedites group movement by doing things for the group, performing routine tasks, for example distributing materials, rearranging seats, operating tape-recorder.
Recorder	Writes down suggestions, makes a record of group decisions; acts as 'group memory'.

GROUP BUILDING AND MAINTENANCE ROLES

Here the analysis of member functions focuses on those contributions that have for their purpose, according to Benne and Sheats, 'the building of group-centred attitudes and orientation among the members of a group or the maintenance and perpetuation of such group-centred behaviour.' A given contribution may involve several roles, and a member or the 'leader' may perform various roles in successive contributions. Here they offered seven categories:

Encourager	Praises, agreed with and accepts the contribution of others; indicates warmth and solidarity in his or her attitude toward other group members; indicates understanding and acceptance of other points of view, ideas and suggestions.
Harmonizer	Mediates the differences between other members; attempts to reconcile disagreements, relieves tension in conflict situations through humour, pouring oil on troubled waters, and so on.
Compromiser	Operates from within a conflict in which his or her idea or position is involved. They may offer compromise by yielding status, admitting their error, by disciplining themselves to maintain group harmony or by 'coming half-way' in moving along with the group.
Gatekeeper-expediter	Attempts to keep communication channels open by encouraging or facilitating the participation of others ('we haven't heard the ideas of Mr X yet', and so on); proposes regulating flow of information, for example

	limits on length of contributions so all can have a say.
Standard setter	Expresses standards for the group or applies standards in evaluating the quality of group process.
Group observer-commentator	Keeps records of various aspects of group process and feeds such data with proposed interpretations into the group's evaluation of its own procedures.
Follower	Goes along with the movement of the group, more or less passively accepting the ideas of others, serving as audience in group discussion and decision.

INDIVIDUAL ROLES

Benne and Sheats included a section on 'individual' roles, emphasizing the word individual with quote marks. They obviously viewed these individual behaviours unfavourably. Attempts by 'members of a group to satisfy individual needs which are irrelevant to the group task and which are non-oriented or negatively oriented to group building and maintenance set problems of groups and member training. A high incidence of "individual-centres" as opposed to "group-centres" participation in a group always calls for self-diagnosis of the group'.

They identified eight such 'unhelpful' individual roles:

Aggressor	Deflates status of others; expresses disapproval of the values, acts or feelings of others; attacks group or the problem it is working on; jokes aggressively; shows envy towards others.

Blocker	Tends to be negative and stubbornly resistant; disagrees and opposes without or beyond reason; attempts to maintain or bring back an issue after the group has rejected or by-passed it.
Recognition-seeker	Works in various ways to call attention to himself or herself: boasting, reporting on personal achievements, acting in unusual ways or struggling to prevent being placed in an 'inferior' position.
Self-confessor	Uses the audience opportunity that the group setting provides to express personal, non-group oriented ideas, feelings and insights.
Playboy	Makes a display of his or her lack of involvement in the group's processes, in the form of cynicism, nonchalance, horseplay and other less studied forms of 'out of school' behaviour.
Dominator	Tries to assert authority of superiority in manipulating the group or certain members of the group, by for example flattery, asserting superior status or right to attention, giving directions authoritatively, interrupting the contributions of others.
Help-seeker	Attempts to call forth 'sympathy' response from other members or the whole group, through expressions of insecurity, personal confusion or depreciation of himself or herself beyond reason.
Special interest pleader	Speaks for the 'small businessman', the 'grass roots' community, the 'housewife', all 'work people' and so on, usually cloaking his or her own prejudices or biases in the stereotype which best fits their individual need.

FUNCTIONS IN PERSPECTIVE

The notes on these roles give you a fair idea of the kind of behaviour that you might have observed if you had been sitting in on one of the American T-groups in the 1950s and 1960s. (T-groups were leaderless groups that were given no other task than to become a group. Initially they were used for research purposes but later became methods of training, hence the 'T'.) Observation of task, group and individual behaviour using the Benne-Sheats forms played a prime part in sensitivity training – sensitivity to the variety of roles and sensitivity to the roles one played oneself and their effects on others.

You can see that although the three headings of 'Task', 'Group' and 'Individual' are already present in embryo, the functions (alias roles) described are very dependent upon the unstructured and so-called 'leaderless' created group setting. In Chapter 6 these functions are developed to accord more with real life situations.

You will have noticed the rather ambivalent overtones concerning the individual in the Group Dynamics movement. Unless he or she is subordinating himself or herself to the group in some way the individual is seen as rather a nuisance. This anti-individualism of Group Dynamics later attracted much criticism from writers such as William H. Whyte, author of the influential book *The Organization Man* (1955).

Psychologists who became prominent prophets in the 1960s – notably A.H. Maslow and Fred Herzberg – joined in the attack. In the next chapter I shall present my own philosophy of groups and persons within them.

When you read the description of 'individual roles' by Benne and Sheats – essentially seen as irrelevant to the group

– you can see why the US schools of social psychology concentrated exclusively on the *task* and *group maintenance* (alias
human relations or socio-emotional behaviour) areas, and
virtually dropped the third area – the *individual* – completely.
Other US theorists, such as Blake and Mouton, Hersey and
Blanchard, worked with this restricted palette of the *two*
dimensions of task and human relations, whereas in the UK
I continued to develop the *three* circles as a whole. In the next
chapter the third dimension – the individual – will be
explored in a much more positive way.

KEY POINTS: MEMBER FUNCTIONS

- Group life can be analysed in several ways. There is the
  distinction between *content* and *process*. Content is what is
  being discussed while process is *how* the group is functioning. Another related but different distinction was between
  behaviour related to the *task* and behaviour related to the
  maintenance of the group and behaviour that merely
  expressed *individual* idiosyncrasies.
- These pioneer studies, in many respects unsatisfactory
  from the viewpoint of today, form the starting point for
  our modern functional understanding of leadership.
- You should practise observation in small groups. The
  categories listed in this chapter can be used for this purpose – providing you do not take them too seriously. Aim
  to become a participant-observer.

*Effective groups develop when each member is contributing
to the common task and to building the group.*

5

THE INDIVIDUAL

'We cannot live only for ourselves. A thousand fibres
connect us with our fellow men; and among those
fibres, as sympathetic threads, our actions come as
causes, and they come back to us as threads.'
*Herman Melville, US writer including
author of* Moby Dick

Groups are, first of all, collections of individuals. An understanding of groups, therefore, has to start with an understanding of individuals. But how do you do that? It could be
argued that it is impossible to understand individuals *in
general* – for that is a contradiction in terms. If you want to
know Bill you must talk to him, study him and read his life
story. No amount of reading books about men in general
will help you. Bill is Bill.

Although that argument is partly true it is also partly false.
For, in its extreme form, it assumes that Bill is *totally* unique.
But in fact, different as Bill is, he shares certain factors or
elements that are common to all other individuals. What are
they?

Here then is the beginning of a strategy for getting to
know individuals. We need: (1) to understand what is

common to all of us, what it can be predicted that all individuals will be or do; and (2) to grasp also what is different, special or in our experience unique about this particular person. The art is to maintain a balance between these two perspectives.

In this chapter I shall present my own philosophy of the person in the group, the relation of group or social life to being an individual.

WHAT IS COMMON TO ALL INDIVIDUALS?

Humans, as we all know, have much in common with animals: the need for food and shelter, security and self-preservation, for instance. For that matter we share some of the characteristics of machines: input of raw materials, conversion to energy and outputs. These two models – animals and machines – do not, however, take us very far into the territory of human nature.

Our social nature has its roots in our evolutionary past and to some extent we share that too with animals. Various species of animals, birds, fish or insects vary in the extent to which they are social. Some creatures live and hunt alone, except for the mating activity. Our nearest relations – gorillas, apes and chimpanzees – are clearly nearer the social end of the spectrum.

Yet when we compare our social behaviour to those of apes there are some marked differences as well as similarities. One observation has especially interested me in this context. Before a child is six months old its mother gives it things to clutch in its tiny hands. Gradually the child begins to play a greater part in this game of exchanging for the sake of exchange. By the year's end the baby is making half of the offerings. Baby gorillas don't do this!

In other words, human mothers naturally evoke their child's distinctive human capacity to give and receive. This reciprocity between persons, signified by the giving and receiving of gifts, takes us a long way forwards. Even before a child has anything of its own to give, its parents give it money or things so that it may buy or make presents to give back to them. It is a game that equips the child for full membership in the human family. The essence of that family life is giving and receiving.

In this social context being a *person* – personality – develops. We are persons before being a *particular* person – alias an individual.

It is impossible to think of a person without this social intercourse of giving and receiving. The exchange of gifts, of course, is symbolic of a deeper willingness to give and receive in society. We come later to give according to our talents and abilities; just as we come to receive according to the abilities of others. We give what we are – just as we may perhaps tend to become what we give.

There is, I submit, a tendency in human nature, strengthened in some children by maladroit parents, to want to take rather than give, or to take more than we give – taking and receiving not being quite the same. This inclination of proclivity is a manifestation of a deeper selfishness that can grip us. Of course, there is a sense in which we have to be selfish or self-centred in order to survive: it is natural to put oneself first, although this is balanced in nature by the 'herd instinct', the desire for the survival of the group or species. But the bias in human nature towards self, which we can see and resent without being able to do much about it, can make us grasping, greedy and covetous in our relationships with others.

There is a conflict between this aspect of human nature not only with the 'herd instinct' factor for corporate rather than individual welfare but also with a natural *moral* law that we perceive, often in a hazy, distorted or fragmented way, in all human relationships. This is the law that giving and receiving should be somehow roughly *equivalent* or equal in value.

There is a special application of this principle of *justice* in criminal matters, summed up in the proverbial phrase: 'An eye for an eye, a tooth for a tooth'. The same principle applies in bartering. Here it is felt that goods traded should be equal in value. With the introduction of money, primarily as a more convenient means of exchange, goods or services bought or sold were supposed to be equal in value to the gold, silver or copper exchanged for them.

Most social psychologists hold the idea that there is some form of psychological contact between an individual and a group, that the rewards of membership will roughly equal the investment (of time talents and so on) the individual makes. Satisfaction is a concept impossible to define precisely but if satisfaction as felt by the individual falls below a certain level he or she will leave the group.

The concept of justice does not exhaust morality; it is only the foundation for human relationships. Being a person leads us to consider the human spirit.

The human spirit is clearly not to be thought of as just one part of our constitution as human beings. Rather it is a way of speaking about that which makes us most truly and fully personal.

The concept of spirit, I suggest, includes the capacity for what could be called self-transcendence. The phrase human spirit is something to do with our extraordinary capacity to reach beyond our limitations, stemming from our consciousness of ourselves as finite, limited individuals. We can, as it were, stand back from ourselves and be aware of ourselves as persons.

One of the deep attractions of teamwork is precisely that membership of a good team does allow us to transcend our own individual limitations of knowledge, ability and performance.

'The joy of working harmoniously with small groups of people who are dedicated to something bigger than themselves, and are completely loyal to each other, counts in my experience as one of the most rewarding things in life', a senior manager once told me. Most of us would agree with him.

That is the first step to transcending self-interest. For this capacity for self-transcendence is to be found mainly in our relations with other people. Your spirit, it has been said, is never as uniquely yours as your body, your life or your individuality. It lives only in relation to some other.

Go back for a moment to that moral balance between giving and receiving. When you love someone there may well be occasions when you transcend the rules. You give where there is no hope of return. The coin in which you are paid is joy, which is not the same as pleasure or gratification but provides a deeper and longer-lasting satisfaction.

In human relations, then, we operate with some notion of justice, in a 'contract' based upon reciprocal and equivalent obligations or responsibilities. But, being persons, we can rise to the call and transcend that contract. Then there is a fuller expression of the human spirit. I love to contemplate that truth: it is so full of hope for the human race.

The concept of being a person in this sense gives us a human right to insist upon being treated as a person – not as an animal, a machine or a thing. We each have an inalienable *dignity* in this sense. We owe it to all persons to require that dignity in us to be at least tacitly accepted or recognized, just as we have to fight if the person in others is being defaced.

Again this constitutes a central moral principle. Take, for

example, the relations between the sexes. The fundamental contract is not 'You treat me as a woman, and I'll treat you as a man', though that in some circumstances is a step forward. Nor can the moral contract be rephrased as: 'You treat me as a person, and I'll treat you as a person'. For a moral person there is no such conditional clause. I *must* treat you as a person, whether you respond in kind or not, because you *are* a person. Therefore treating you as a thing – manipulating or using you in any way – will never work, at least in the long run.

These principles about all persons, rather than particular persons, strike me as important in the context of effective teambuilding and leadership for this reason. Your *attitudes* stem ultimately from what beliefs, perceptions or assumptions you hold about human nature. If you get your fundamental picture of man and woman wrong, then a degree of falsity will eventually colour your derived attitudes to people at work. You may wish to challenge the view I have expressed here. But I hope that at least my words will have stimulated you to think out your own concept of human nature, so that you are clearer about your values. For if your vision of man is flawed or inadequate, you can be sure that people will become aware of it. Then no accumulation of 'interpersonal skills' or 'behavioural techniques' will save the day for you.

DEVELOPING AS PERSONS

Your characteristics as a person are not wholly determined by the action of the environment; they are also shaped by who you are within yourself as a unique person. Your inheritance provides you with a given nature and potential. The dialogue between you and the world is also to be understood as a dialogue between heredity and environment.

In personal terms some of the early elements in that dialogue
– in family and school – might be:

Sense of trust	Trust towards oneself and towards others, as receiving and giving develops. Significant communication does not occur until some relationship of trust is established.
Sense of autonomy	A child needs the constant care, supervision and love of his parents; on the other hand, he needs to assert his will and stand over against his parents as a separate person. He needs to be part of others and distinct from them, to belong and yet to be self-sufficient.
Sense of initiative	A child must find out what kind of person he or she is going to be. Their search will be helped if they have been encouraged to develop a sense of initiative. It is the power that moves people to begin things.
Sense of industry	Playing, schoolwork and membership of teams at school can develop a sense of industry. Vocational work – the principal contribution of adults – is central to personal life.
Sense of integrity	Integrity means first learning to adhere to standards or values outside oneself. This gives life reference points other than self-interest. It aids the development of wholeness.
Sense of security	People like and need a sense of security that comes from understanding where they stand in relation to the other significant people in their lives.

INDIVIDUALS AND INDIVIDUALISTS

Individuals are just particular persons. The word individual has gone through a revolution of meaning. Coming from the Latin *individuus*, meaning indivisible, it was once used to emphasize that we are joined together: as individuals we are inseparable. Now it stresses the exact opposite, namely that each person is an indivisible whole, existing as a distinct entity.

The contemporary emphasis on our individuality, the total character that is peculiar to an individual and distinguishes them from others, has been fed by a number of cultural trends and tides in the West: religious, educational and artistic. In my book *Management and Morality* (1974) and again in *Founding Fathers: The Puritans in England and America* (1984) I discussed the history of the concept of the individual and I shall not repeat myself here. One feature of Japan, a society immune from these influences until the middle of the last century, is the much greater prominence there of society, organization and group and the relatively low development of the concept of individuality. That situation, of course, is changing as Western influences take effect.

An over-emphasis on the individual can be as harmful to effective teamwork as an over-emphasis on the group. For it leads to *individualism* – the philosophy that the interests of the individual are or ought to be ethically paramount, coupled sometimes with the doctrine that all values, rights and duties originate in individuals. This in turn leads to a concentration on promoting the political and economic independence of the individual. The watchwords are individual initiative, action and interests. This ideology of individualism is based upon a half-truth: it ignores the other half of the picture, that we are all 'members one of another'. As the English religious poet Francis Quarles expressed it:

No man is born unto himself alone;
Who lives unto himself, he lives to none

These movements within our culture, towards recognizing the dignity of each person and developing both our common and our peculiar characteristics through education, has made us all more self-conscious of our individuality. Sometimes that heightened awareness is accompanied by a sense of cosmic loneliness. Alexander Selkirk – the real-life castaway prototype of Robinson Crusoe – voiced that feeling in William Cowper's poem: 'I am out of humanity's reach, I must finish my journey alone'.

Most of us are not so out of love with humanity that we should deliberately choose to isolate ourselves from others. Some people do. For them freedom is necessary in order to be an individual. Therefore they are fleeing the constraints of group membership, mindless of its rewards.

Henry David Thoreau, the US writer who took to living alone in the wilderness of a hundred years ago, wrote: 'Wherever a man goes, other men will pursue him and paw him with their dirty institutions, and if they can, will constrain him to belong to their desperate oddfellow society'.

The extreme individualist, in the first sense as one who advocates and practises individualism, is obviously going to find it difficult to work as a member of a team. For team membership involves a contract to put the interests of the whole team before one's own, at least for the duration of a task. If the group's interests conflict with his or her own – or any other individual's for that matter – he or she will invariably put the rights of the individual first. The natural tendency for communities and organizations peopled by such individualists is towards fragmentation. In the early colonial days of America, for example, such individualists were allowed to go and settle in what is now the state of

Rhode Island, where they predictably made heavy weather of governing themselves.

Working groups, communities and organizations, however, should be able to accommodate individualists in the second sense of that word: those who pursue a markedly independent course in thought and action. For creative people – artists and scientists, inventors and leaders – tend to be individualists within this meaning of the word.

It is not easy to lead or manage individualists, nor is it easy for individualists to submit themselves to being managed or led by others. They are far more likely to respond to good leaders – leaders they respect and trust – than to being managed in a systematic, routine or bureaucratic way. They of all people need to be treated as individuals – the subject of the next section.

Apart from the way they are treated, what attracts the individualist into a working group and what sustains him or her while they are in it?

In order to answer the first question we must go back for a moment to the concept of reciprocity, the giving and receiving that expresses and builds up personality.

SHARING

Giving and receiving implies a two-fold model of relationship. In the 'Two-way relationship' diagram below the two people concerned are metaphorically gazing into each other's eyes:

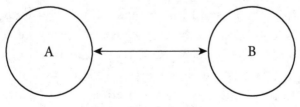

Two-way relationship

But there is a third concept, which might be called *sharing*. The two people in the 'Sharing' diagram below are metaphorically gazing together towards a third object or person. They see each other, so to speak, out of the corners of their eyes; they come closer together as they move towards the common object of interest.

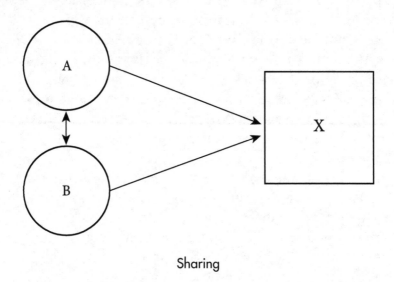

Sharing

Giving and receiving between A and B still occurs in the three-fold model but it happens within the context of the common interest, task or area of concern X. If you have a passion for stamp collecting, for example, you may give and receive gifts of specimens – or barter them with a fellow enthusiast in your stamp club, or you may simply swap ideas on how to conserve and display your collection.

Even the most devout individualist can therefore be drawn into the social life of cooperation when he or she discovers that someone else – perhaps an equally ardent individualist – shares his or her particular interest. This mental discovery of common ground is often the moment of conception for a lasting friendship.

If X has sufficient value for them, then, A and B may well be willing to accept a limit on their individual freedoms in order to pursue successfully and together the object of their common desire.

The first condition for free persons to cooperate is this perception of value in the common task. It has to be worthwhile. The second factor – the one that can sustain an individualist in a group or team – is the ability to internalize discipline: to transform the constraints that the common task and the need to work together impose into self-discipline. This seems to me the only way of reconciling two apparent opposites. For self-discipline implies constraint but because it is self-imposed you remain free – no one is doing it to you. Hence the English poet John Milton's exhortation: 'Love virtue, she alone is free'.

This virtue, this self-discipline, not only transforms the experience of social or technical constraints but also transcends their demands. The minimum limitations on individual freedom are commonly expressed in the form of codes of laws or rules, some unwritten. A self-disciplined individual will both fulfil and sometimes transcend these rules. A naturally courteous person, for example, will sometimes say more or do more than the conventions of etiquette or good manners require. He or she is seen to be free although they have in fact subjected themselves to a demanding principle.

Can individualists work in groups and teams? Yes, provided they see sufficient value in the common task and that co-operative effort is more likely to produce results than individual effort. That rational argument needs to be won. But they will not sustain their place in working teams unless they are prepared to discipline themselves to accept – and perhaps go beyond – the standards of the group. Such self-discipline, however, carries an attractive bonus. For it maintains personal freedom, the reverse face of individuality.

ON TREATING PEOPLE AS INDIVIDUAL PERSONS

We are all individuals, though not all of us are individualists. Groups and organizations that treat their members as individuals are more likely to be successful than those that treat them as a set of numbers. But what does the cry 'please, *please*, treat me as an individual' really mean?

The recognition that every person, like every situation, is unique is the foundation of the necessary attitude. There are naturally similarities between us – of needs, temperament, interest, habit, job, and so on – but in each of us the similarity is qualified in a peculiar way. You and I may both have a sense of humour but it will be a different sense of humour and the differences will be apparent to both us and our friends as we come to know each other well.

As a manager, you are like tens of thousands of other managers, and yet you are relatively different. That is, if you are to act and be acted upon in the most fruitful way, the best being drawn out from you and the best being given to you, you must regard yourself and be regarded by others in your individuality.

When regarded simply as a manager (or an operative) you become merely a specimen of a kind. One of the paradoxes of modern life is that while the claims of individuality are more frequently and more vociferously voiced than ever before, we are organizing ourselves more busily along lines that suppress individuality. In one group after another we are being persuaded, cajoled, trapped or pressured into suppressing our initiative, judgement and responsibility. Many people are ceasing to have either power or significance except as a member of this group or that. We have compressed our complex individuality into the areas where we conform and resemble others.

Liberation from such incipient group or organizational tyranny only comes when the individual is recognized, grasped and accepted in his or her individuality as well as his or her humanity and personhood. That includes an appreciation of the unique contribution that *this* person can make both to common task and common life.

EXERCISE: Spot the difference
Select any individual you know well and list the ways in which they *differ* from other persons under the following headings:

Temperament	Perception
Attitudes	Beliefs
Abilities	Motivation
Values	Skills
Knowledge	Character
Intelligence	Creativity
History	Background

It has been said that an adult has tens of thousands of beliefs, hundreds of attitudes, but only dozens of values. Do you agree?

Reflections of a cricket captain

Mike Brearley, one of England's most successful cricket captains, reflects here on the need to balance individual and group interest in the team. How do you build a team of individualists?

Cricket is a team game, but as such it is unusual in being made up of intensely individual duels. Personal interest may conflict with that of the team: you may feel exhausted, and yet have to bowl, you may be required to sacrifice your wicket going for quick runs. And these conflicting tensions can easily give rise to the occupational vice of cricket – selfishness.

The drive for personal success is vital to the team. Without it, a player can fail to value himself, and assume a diffidence which harms the team. He might, for example, under-rate the importance to his confidence – and thus to the team's long-term interest – of his occupying the crease for hours, however boringly, in a search for form. And I have seen a whole side in flight from selfishness, with batsmen competing to find more ridiculous ways of getting themselves out in order to prove that they weren't selfish.

It is the captain's job to coax the happy blend of self-interest and team interest from his players, influencing the balance between individual and group. Thus he enables the group to create and sustain its identity without a deadening uniformity, and to enable the individuals to express themselves as fully as possible without damaging the interest of the whole.

Ian Botham, Brearley's successor as Captain of the England Cricket XI, said of him: 'There is something about the man. He reads me like a book. He knows what I am thinking and gets the best out of me'. It is this ability to understand each individual – each part that makes up the whole – that made Brearley such an outstanding leader.

KEY POINTS: THE INDIVIDUAL

• An individual is a particular person. Being fully a person means that he or she is capable of giving and receiving. We have notions of what is fair, namely an equivalence in this mutual exchange. But, possessed of the human spirit, we can transcend these moral ideas of justice in personal relationships.

- We give according to our unique pattern of talents, abilities or gifts. Slowly we discover what they are. But we should be nothing if others did not receive our gifts. Where would Mozart be if no musicians gave him their skills or no audiences gave him their attention?

- Achieving a balance between the interests and self-expression of each individual on the one hand and of the group on the other is one of the most challenging tasks of leaders. It is best done by reference to the third dimension – the common task. For it is the value of this task that draws us together and underpins our unity.

- Team members need to know when to be very supportive and sensitive, and when to challenge and be tough.

- Your attitudes are more fundamental to your success in teambuilding than any skills or techniques. They stem from your values. Explore your values and keep them in good repair.

- When a team is working perfectly, people play to each other's strengths and cover each other's weaknesses.

Let us rejoice in our individuality, but let us be sure that we develop it for the benefit of others.

6

THREE INTERLOCKING NEEDS IN GROUP LIFE

'The language of truth is simple.'
German proverb

'A picture is worth a thousand words', says the Chinese proverb. In this chapter I want to pull together with the help of a picture – the three circles – the threads of the preceding five chapters.

In my previous books on leadership I have advanced one general theory about working groups and organizations. Apart from being the only general theory in the field it has proved extremely fruitful as the basis for leadership training. More than one million managers have now been through courses based upon it.

This theory begins with the proposition that all groups (like persons) are individuals. Even groups in the same organization develop after a time what Lord Attlee referring to British Cabinets called 'a group personality'. For that reason what works in one group may not work in another. But groups share certain common needs. In this chapter we shall explore those needs and their implications for teams and leaders.

WHAT NEEDS ARE PRESENT IN THE LIFE
OF EVERY GROUP?

The needs of the group can be summarized as follows:

Task   The need to accomplish something – build a
               house, sing an anthem, determine a budget, plan
               a conference, solve a problem, climb a mountain.
               The need of the group is to try to accomplish this
               task. So long as this task remains undone, there
               will be a tension in the group and an urge to
               complete the task. The task is *what* the group is
               talking about or working on. The task is usually
               seen in terms of *things* rather than people.

Group   The need to develop and maintain working
               relationships among the members so that the
               group task can be accomplished. This is called
               the maintenance need of the group. Maintenance
               refers primarily to *people* and their relationships
               with each other. It concerns *how* people relate to
               each other *as* they work at the group task. Unless
               members listen to each other, for example, and
               try to build upon each other's suggestions it will
               be very difficult, and often impossible, for the
               group to accomplish its task. Yet maintenance is
               frequently neglected in groups. How long would
               a fleet of jet airliners be able to operate if they
               were not serviced, refuelled and otherwise
               maintained?

Individual   The needs of individuals come with them into
               groups. People work in groups not only because
               of interest in the task to be accomplished but also
               because membership of groups fulfils their
               various needs. Why do people work in the first

place? They work because they are hungry, they are thirsty and they need somewhere to sleep. Even today, when we use money as a means of exchange, most of our salary goes in satisfying those basic needs. But a satisfied need ceases to motivate. Once you have enough food and drink, once you have a house, other needs rise up in the human heart. You become interested in a pension, job security and safety of work. If those security needs are satisfied by good company policy and through the welfare state, people do not then turn round and say, 'Thank you, we are now fully satisfied'. Instead they discover other areas of need bubbling up within them: the quality of relationships in working life; respect from others and self-respect; and then the need for 'self-actualization', a fulfilment of one's potential by growth. The needs for physical satisfaction and security are stronger and more deep-rooted; if they are threatened then we jump back and defend them. The needs for self-esteem, the respect of others and self-fulfilment are weaker, but they are more distinctively human. If such needs can be met *along with* and not *at the expense of* the group task and maintenance needs, then the group will tend to be more effective.

As you will see from the 'Three areas of need' diagram opposite, the three circles overlap. If you achieve the common task, the effects will flow into the group circle and help to create a sense of unity. And they will also influence the individual circle. In fact you can work round the diagram. If you have a good group, for example, you are more likely to achieve the task. If the individuals concerned are fully involved and motivated, then they are going to give much more to the task and much more to the group. By contrast, if you imagine a black circle totally eclipsing the task circle that would symbolize a total failure of the task area. You would then have taken quite a chunk out of the group area, and a similar one out of the individual circle too. If you could put that black circle over the group maintenance area, then again it would show that lack of group cohesiveness will affect the other two circles.

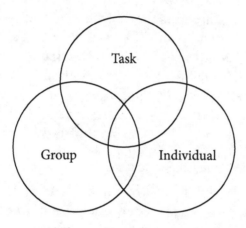

Three areas of need

NEEDS AND LEADERSHIP FUNCTIONS

In order that the task and maintenance needs should be met, certain *functions* have to be performed. A function is what you do as opposed to a quality or trait.

In Chapter 4, I listed the 'roles' or functions introduced by Benne and Sheats in the late 1940s. Observers in Group Dynamics training laboratories found these rather long; moreover we found it difficult to use two separate forms at once. Therefore various efforts were made to produce a composite list.

One such working categorization, suggested by Gibb and Gibb in *Applied Group Dynamics* (National Training Laboratories) influenced my subsequent efforts. They indicated five broad categories of leadership functions:

Initiating   Keeping the group action moving, or getting it going (for example, suggesting action step, pointing out goal, proposing procedure, clarifying).

Regulating   Influencing the direction and tempo of the group's work (for example, summarizing, pointing out time limits, restating goal).

Informing   Bringing information or opinion to the group.

Supporting   Creating an emotional climate that holds group together, makes it easy for members to contribute to work on the task (for example, harmonizing, relieving tension, voicing group feeling, encouraging).

Evaluation   Helping the group to evaluate its decisions, goals or procedures (for example, testing for consensus, noting group process).

A group needs all five of these types of function if it is to accomplish its task and maintain its cohesiveness. Early in a group's work initiating functions are much needed. Later, as solutions are proposed, informing and regulating functions may assume much more importance. Supporting functions are needed all the way along. The evaluating function becomes especially relevant as the group nears the end of its work. Group work will be effective, then, to the degree that needed group functions are supplied at the time they are needed.

SOME IMPLICATIONS

Sooner or later all three kinds of needs present in every group must be met to some extent in order to achieve effectiveness and satisfaction. When needed functions are missing, group progress is slow and uneven.

This does *not* imply that at every moment exactly one third of the group's attention and energy should be devoted to each of these three kinds of needs. Over a period of time there may be great fluctuations in the amount of group attention and energy directed to any one of these needs. The amount of energy to be allocated depends upon the ability of the members to diagnose which of the three needs is most pressing at every moment, and their ability to meet this perceived need.

The performing of one function may help to meet two or even three needs simultaneously.

Most people usually have preferences for providing one or another function most often, such as the inveterate summarizer, hence the tendency to use the word 'role' in the context of group life. But most people can at least potentially make more than one functional contribution.

KEY POINTS: THREE INTERLOCKING NEEDS IN GROUP LIFE

- Always bear in mind the 'Three areas of need' as depicted in the three circles model. It is a simple sketch map of working group life. If and when a group bogs down, look for a needed but missing function, and then perform it or encourage someone else to perform it.
- Through training (which includes observation and prac-

tice) you can learn to perform skilfully a wide variety of useful member functions.

- Skill is technique that has been mastered to the point where you do not have to think about it. In working groups it consists of knowing *what* to say and do, *when*, and *how.*
- The skilfulness of your participation is to be judged more by its *effect* upon the group than by your own intentions.

Acquiring skill is learning to bring behaviour into line with your intentions.

7

GROUP PROCESSES

'In a personal relation between persons an impersonal
element is necessarily included and subordinated.'
John MacMurray, British philosopher

Process issues, you may recall, revolve around the underlying
ways in which a group works. Again, to repeat an earlier
point, it is not the same as group maintenance. In this and
the following chapter I shall draw out some more lessons
about group processes that are relevant to teamwork today.

In order to clothe the rather nebulous concept of process
I have chosen three examples: responses to authority, response
to frustration and decision making procedures. These are obviously not directly connected with each other. Taken together,
however, they can lead us some steps further in understanding
more fully what goes on in groups.

In each section you should bear in mind the Group
Dynamics provenance for these ideas. But I have selected
these particular instances of group process because I have
experienced them many times in working groups and I have
found the work of psychologists here illuminating rather
than obfuscating.

PROCEDURES

All groups need to use some procedures – ways of working – to get things done. In formal business meetings, we are accustomed to a set of rules or procedures. Informal groups usually use less rigid procedures. The choice of procedures has a direct effect on such other aspects of group life as atmosphere, participation and cohesion. Choosing procedures that are appropriate to the situation and the work to be done may require a degree of flexibility and inventiveness by a group.

CHECKLIST:
Group procedures

- How does the group determine its practices or agenda?
- How does it make decisions – by vote, silent assent or consensus?
- How does it discover and make use of the resources of its members?
- How does the work of various members, subgroups and activities get coordinated?
- How does the group evaluate its work?

DECISION MAKING

Group processes revolve around the core of decision making. How are decisions made? Or do they just happen? That is a central issue for groups.

Take the case of a group of doctors working together in a primary health care team in Bristol. There are four doctors, together with district nurses and health visitors, making up this team. The senior partner is a woman aged 51, and the other doctors – all men – are aged 29, 32 and 35. At one meeting the younger doctors proposed that if disagreements arose about matters concerning the group practice, decisions should be taken by vote. The senior partner put her foot down and insisted that decisions should be by consensus. Do you think she was right to do so?

Decisions occur – or do not, as the case may be – by a variety of methods. Here you will see group processes at work in the following ways:

Apathy	Nobody is sufficiently interested or concerned to get the group to operate, that is, deciding not to decide by tacit agreement.
Plops	A decision suggested by an individual to which there is no response. Plopping often occurs in a new group confronted by many problems; in a group where a number of the members have fairly equal status; when a member is overly aggressive; when a member has difficulty in articulating.
Self-authorized decisions	A decision made by an individual who assumes authority to do so. When such a decision is proposed, the group as a whole often finds it easier to accept than reject, even though some individuals may not be in agreement. The decision is thus by default.
Pairing	A decision made by two members of the group joining forces. Such 'hand-clasping' sometimes emerges so suddenly that it catches the other members of the group off guard and at the same time presents them with another problem (how to deal with the two people at once).

Topic-jumping   A decision to cut short by the inappropriate intrusion of another topic. Topic-jumping confuses the issue confronting the group and thus changes the nature of the decision.

Minority group   A decision agreed upon in advance by several members of the group. Cliques are present in almost every group, and their prearranged decision may be very good. But the effect of collusion can be to destroy group cohesiveness and a sense of trust.

Minority views   A decision made by some form of voting. The traditional procedure of taking a vote often seems to be the only way in which to reach a decision under the given circumstances. Nonetheless the minority may remain against the decision despite the vote and therefore not likely to act on it.

Does anyone disagree?   A decision made by pressure not to disagree. When confronted by such a question, several persons who really disagree strongly or who have not had the opportunity to express their opinion on the issue, might show real reluctance to voice opposition with no apparent support.

Note that the 'Ways of reaching a decision' diagram opposite includes *true consensus* and *false consensus*. In the latter everyone *appears* to agree but when the decision is acted upon, each member seems to have different ideas about the decision or to have reserved the right not to implement it. Some members may have only pretended to agree in the first place, hoping the matter would be forgotten or that the decision could subsequently be fudged.

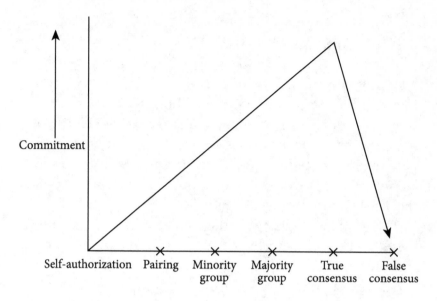

Ways of reaching a decision

True consensus is not always possible even if it is normally desirable because it can be very time-consuming. It occurs when communication has been sufficiently open for all to feel they have had a fair chance to influence the decision and the 'feeling of the meeting' emerges without voting. The following definition is worth bearing in mind:

> When alternatives have been debated thoroughly by the group and everyone is prepared to accept that in the circumstances one particular solution is the best way forward, even though it might not be *every* person's preferred solution.
>
> The most important test is that everyone is prepared to *act* as though it was their preferred solution.

RESPONSES TO AUTHORITY

Not all the processes at work below the surface – or on it – in group life are concerned with making decisions or constitute procedures for tackling common goals. Under the umbrella of group processes we can look at two recurring patterns in group life: the different responses to the leader's authority and the tendency of groups to withdraw or 'take flight' when faced with difficulty.

The T-group began with the trainer asking the group to 'become a group' and then sitting back, apparently leaving them to their own devices.

This overt behaviour – apparently a complete abdication from the leadership role – sparked off several reactions in groups that in time became fairly predictable. Although conditioned and sharpened by the T-group environment, they are latent in all of us and you will have experienced some of them in daily life at work in certain situations. The first pair, for example, would be recognized by most of us in our family roles as children and parents:

Dependency	Members look to others to tell them what to do. They are completely dependent upon the 'authority figure' and are lost without them.
Counter-dependency	Members resist authority, especially from the leader. They are hostile to any attempt to curtail their freedom. 'What right have you got to tell me what to do?'

The *dependency* and *counter-dependency* phases we go through as children in regard to our parents and teachers can get fixed. There are adults who carry around with them these latent attitudes towards those in authority.

The dependent person clearly needs to be nurtured – coaxed, counselled and coached – into taking a less dependent stance in regard to authority. It is not easy because the pattern of dependency can be stamped on a person's nature by parents and teachers.

In dealing with counter-dependence it is important to realize first that these hostile, frustrated feelings are not being directed at you personally. They are often the by-product left in the human soul of over-dominant parents or autocratic teachers. In weaning someone from counter-dependency you should not parade your authority; your legitimate authority should stem from your knowledge and personality.

In emerging from these two states (and counter-dependency can be the flipside of dependency) we have to go through the stage of *independence*. The independent person is neither dependent nor counter-dependent to a leader. The adjective carries good overtones of autonomy and freedom.

Independence can also mean: 'I am going to have nothing to do with you'. In this case the person severs himself from the offending source of authority, if need be by force or flight. This may be necessary if that authority has tried to keep you under tight rein or is authoritarian in his or her behaviour. Otherwise independence is a natural phase of growing up.

Yet it is not the end of the story. For independence in the second sense contravenes the elementary principle of reciprocity: that we are made for, and made in, a fundamental process of giving and receiving. The natural end of our striving, then, is the stage of *interdependence*, the social commerce of free and equal individuals who accept that their skills, natures and needs are complementary.

FIGHT AND FLIGHT

When faced with a difficulty, especially one that is threatening, humans can either stand their ground and fight or they can take flight. This behaviour can be categorized as follows:

Fighting and dominating	Disagreeing; asserting personal dominance; attacking whatever is believed to be responsible for the cause of stress. It is common, for example, to blame others – individuals, groups, institutions or ideas.
Flight and withdrawal	Staying out of discussion; daydreaming; sulking; running away physically or psychologically.
Pairing	In pairing, individuals seek reassurance from other individuals about their feelings of anxiety or discomfort.

But sometimes the whole group may take a fighting stance. Doubtless you can think of groups who have become belligerent. What is not so obvious, however, is when a group is *taking flight* in a psychological way from a dangerous area.

You may notice symptoms include a higher degree of rather artificial play acting or 'larking about'. Nervous humour and jokes are often symptoms of tension, for laughter is a safety valve. This is why groups often laugh at jokes or remarks that are not really funny.

An intriguing method of group flight occurs when the discussion shifts from the particular to the *general* – and stays there. It can be a form of flight, for example, to discuss the 'problem of leadership today' rather than tackle the central issue in the group, which is: 'You, Jack, are not giving us any leadership'.

It is of course not always true that groups who are talking in general or theoretical terms are evading some problems within their own life. Sometimes their very reason for being there is to explore such areas in an intellectual fashion. But you should be able to judge when it is flight into the general or abstract. As a form of veering away mentally from a problem or difficulty they should be tackling, it can afflict all groups in all places.

DEFENCE MECHANISMS

The flight into abstract or general discourse is an example of a largely unconscious group response (although a cunning member may manipulate the discussion in that direction if he or she wants no decision to be taken). But individuals also develop unconscious responses to anxiety-making situations. Some of them get 'institutionalized' in their psychological make-up. These can sometimes help to explain why a person may be acting or reacting in a certain way.

One important group are the so-called defence mechanisms. The identification of them was one of the more useful outcomes of Sigmund Freud's work. Defence mechanisms, he believed, are employed by individuals to reduce or overcome anxiety. They provide some insights into human behaviour in groups, as seen overleaf.

It is unwise to play the role of amateur psychologist if you are a leader or manager, for a little learning is a dangerous thing. But Freud's categories can sometimes throw light on the thought-processes or behaviour of individuals in relationships. It may be, too, that groups that have been together for a time will also develop their own defence mechanisms. They also may displace, repress, over-react, project and form fixations. In other words, these can be group as well as individual phenomena. As always, the price of freedom is eternal vigilance.

Displacement	For example, where a team member is annoyed at his or her boss and punishes their own team members or some other person.
Repression	A process by which unacceptable desires or impulses are excluded from consciousness and left to operate in the unconscious, for example, where an individual blocks out or represses an unpleasant experience.
Regression	Reversion to an earlier mental or behavioural level, for example, when an adult behaves in a childish fashion.
Over-reaction	For example, becoming excessively bureaucratic or rule-abiding.
Projection	The act of externalizing or objectifying what is primarily subjective, for example, projecting one's own thoughts or desires onto others.
Fixation	An obsessive or unhealthy preoccupation or attachment, for example, a persistent concentration on a supposed threat or enemy.
Sublimation	Directing the energy of (an impulse) from its primitive aim to one that is ethically or culturally higher; for example, a naturally aggressive person who becomes an attacking hockey centre forward.

Some depth mind strategies

KEY POINTS: GROUP PROCESSES

- With practice of observation, using this book as a guide, you should be able to distinguish between the *content* of group discussion and the *process* of group life. Look below the surface and ask yourself 'what is going on here'.
- Decisions will be influenced by group or individual processes that are not immediately apparent. Improved decision making will emerge from a clearer understanding of these pressures and allowing for their effects. Self-awareness is the key.
- Attitudes to authority in general – dependence and counterdependence – can influence the way that group members respond to your leadership. Keep calm. Conduct yourself so as to make it easier for the group and each individual within it to move towards *interdependence* – with you and each other.
- Escapism into dreams or fantasy is no bad thing sometimes – we all do it. But a group that takes flight from the 'here and now' into abstractions, sustained endlessly by psychological filibustering, is never likely to be effective.
- Consensus is a valuable goal in decision making. Where members know each other well, share values and can spend time in discussion together, it should be the rule. But where these factors are not present it is not always possible for a leader to find it.

By understanding what goes on within groups you can learn to work with the grain rather than against it.

PART TWO

BUILDING AND MAINTAINING HIGH-PERFORMANCE TEAMS

'There are four people who should be the hub of the wheel in my factory', said Michael Dix, production director of a factory making shoes. 'The problem is that the organizational structure makes them look like four separate apples hanging on a tree. The chart doesn't say that they have to be a team but that is what this business requires them to be'. He was referring to the raw materials buyer, production planner, market forecaster and distribution manager. 'They are all affected by whatever each one does. If they can't work as a team, then I know only too well what will happen to our narrow profit margins'.

The same is true in every walk of life. Chartered accountant audit teams, on-site project groups, film crews, operating theatre teams, all require talented individual specialists who have acquired the desire and ability to work effectively together in teams.

This need becomes greater in the fast-changing world where the permanent teams at board or operational level, or in the functional areas such as management services, are complemented by numerous temporary task groups in matrix-type organizations. These can increase your flexible response to change; they can stimulate creativity, innovation and productivity within the organization. These teams form, disperse and reform. How can such matrix organizations work as teams? How do you equip yourself with the necessary teambuilding skills? Part Two is designed to help you to answer these questions.

It is relatively easy to establish a degree of teamwork or cooperation between a group of people; it is infinitely harder to develop a high-performance team. In Part Two we are concerned with identifying the factors that go into the making and sustaining of such teams.

To achieve excellence in results over a period of time in an organization, as in a football team, is not accidental. The various properties of groups identified in Part One – communication, decision making, cohesiveness, morale, atmosphere, standards, procedures – are all found again in high-performance teams but to different degrees. The average work group and the exceptional team can be compared to two horses: both have the same muscles, legs, lungs and other organs. But one is an ordinary riding horse in the local stables, the other is a three times winner of the Grand National. Why is one different from the other?

In the transformations of a work group into a team, and an ordinary team into a high-performance team, attention must be given to three crucially important elements: leadership, membership and common methods or strategies of working together.

Teams need good leadership, but high-performance teams need very good leadership. What do we mean by good/very good in this context? What is this scale of merit? In my companion book *Effective Leadership* I introduced the distinction between leaders for good and 'good leaders'. Hitler, for example, was a 'good leader' in the sense that he could inspire people to follow him but he was the archetypal misleader – leading people in the wrong direction. Here I shall assume that the leader's ends are good and concentrate on good leadership in the second sense, namely *have the appropriate skills to lead effectively.*

The same distinction, incidentally, applies to teams. Doubtless the teamwork of those responsible for exterminating millions of Jews in the Second World War in the concentration camps was of a very high order but the ends towards which their cooperative efforts worked were wholly evil.

Personally, to continue the diversion for a moment, I do not believe these two meanings of the word good can ultimately be separated. My reasons for believing this can be detected in the concept of the person outlined in Chapter 5 – the individual.

If we are indeed basically moral as humans then we cannot give ourselves forever to immoral purposes. The structure of reality works against us, slowly perhaps but always inexorably. In the longer term the leader for bad (and the team for bad) will not survive.

In the high-performance team, the personal qualities of the leader complement his or her functional skills in the task and group areas. Not only will he or she provide direction and build the team, they will also add a subtle touch of inspiration.

The ability to inspire others is a general characteristic of good leaders. It is especially important if the group or organization is working in difficult conditions or adverse circumstances, where morale can easily fall. Hitler could recognize this quality of leadership in others intuitively, doubtless because he possessed it so abundantly himself. In deciding to appoint Rommel to command the Afrika Korps in 1941 he said:

> I picked up Rommel because he knows how to *inspire* his troops. This is absolutely essential for the commander of a force that has to fight under particularly arduous climatic conditions like North Africa.

If we ask, 'Why did such-and-such a group or organization, which was perfectly ordinary, become a high-performance team or an excellent organization?', the answer is often that they were *inspired* to raise their sights and standards by the vision, enthusiasm and drive of a particular leader. Therefore it is impossible to divorce effective teambuilding from effective leadership.

The drawback of putting too much emphasis on the leader is that it seems to diminish the role of being a member. The normal counterpart of being a leader is being a follower. We are not ashamed to call ourselves followers of an outstanding leader (Jews, Christians and Muslims are all disciples or followers of Moses, Jesus and the Prophet Mohammed) but, in the context of industry, being a follower strikes some people as being not an appropriate image. Being a team member sounds much more positive.

Membership – this second ingredient in effective teamwork – is best approached through the concept of role. Much of the early theorizing about roles in groups either concentrated upon trivial roles that people assume in groups or roles that people are assigned by group members, such as 'know all' or 'father figure'. Or it personified particular functions (as we saw in the Benne-Sheats lists in Chapter 4).

We are left, then, with two positive roles open to colleagues in a group, those of *leader* and *team member*. We must reject the idea that leadership (in the sense of the provision of task, team and individual functions) is a cake, and the more share the leader has, the less cake there will be for the members. As one very good leader, the chief executive of an electronics engineering company, said to me, 'I have never had so much authority until I started giving it away'.

The idea that there is a team member role, complementary rather than antithetical to the leader's role, and equally positive, is a novel one. What is the content of it? In a high performance team, apart from the all-important specialist roles, the team members' general role consists of being the kind of person able to provide functions to achieve the task, build and maintain the team and develop or encourage other individuals. In a low-grade team a given individual may be good at one or two of these functions only, such as evaluating or summarizing – hence the tendency to label them 'roles' and personify them; he or she will lack the range and flexibility of a really good team member.

For in a high productivity team the social competence of members is such that they can turn their hands to many functions. They are thoroughly flexible, not putting themselves or others into the straitjackets of 'role' definitions.

In this respect leadership and membership so conceived are remarkably similar. But this should cause us no surprise. Moreover it is an asset, for managers are both leaders in one situation and team members (subordinates and colleagues) in others. Such an understanding should enable them to change hats without a crashing of gears, to mix metaphors.

Where leaders and team members differ in role is that the latter are more likely to continue special responsibilities – technical or professional – with their team membership role than are leaders. The roles of leader and member do not exist in a vacuum. They are always combined with other roles; the leader is also manager, doctor, head of department, commanding officer, bishop, and so on. The team member, following that order, may be computer specialist, anaesthetist, admissions tutor, signals officer or archdeacon. In the team context he or she will contribute more than the leader in his or her technical/professional role. There is a sense in which the role of leader is to ensure that everyone else in the team is effectively performing *their* roles.

For leaders and members to blend together to produce results of excellence in their field, a third element – common methods or strategies for doing things – is necessary. A football team needs its well-rehearsed drills. A first-rate musical concert is the product of a competent inspiring conductor, an orchestra of outstanding instrumentalists who are working together as a team, and, thirdly, a common score, such as Mozart's Symphony No. 21.

This analogy breaks down at a certain point, for the equivalent in industry to Mozart's score is the plan that the team itself formulates or implements. It is often composer or author, writing its own script, as well as actor. But it needs some sketchmap, some frame of reference that will help it to interpret what it is doing and give it some method of diagnosing failure. A better comparison would be a science research laboratory, where the scientists and technicians engaged in different activities would all subscribe to scientific method, a system for testing and recording discovery, which can be described and to some extent broken down into its constituent parts.

There is no one equivalent to the scientific method in teamwork generally. But I believe that a combination of the three circles model – the 'Three areas of need' – and a framework for decision making, problem solving and innovative thinking represents a minimum requirement. If not the musical score itself, these components represent the means of setting out the music.

The elements of leader, member and shared processes are the subject of chapters in Part Two.

8

TEALS

'When spiders' webs unite, they can tie up a lion.'
Ethiopian proverb

What is a team? What makes a *good* team? These are simple questions and we tend to think we know the answers – until someone asks!

The word 'team' is often used loosely, sometimes merely as a synonym for group. But strictly speaking there are no synonyms in the English language. A team can be distinguished from a group. Or rather, in the words of Bernard Babington Smith in *Training in Small Groups*, a team is:

> a group in which the individuals have a common aim and in which the jobs and skills of each member fit in with those of others, as – to take a very mechanical and static analogy – in a jigsaw puzzle pieces fit together without distortion and together produce some overall pattern.

The two strands in this definition – a common task and complementary contributions – are essential to the concept of a team. An *effective* team may be defined as one that achieves its aim in the most efficient way and is then ready to take on more challenging tasks if so required.

THE COMMON AIM

The first questions a person – potential leader or member – should ask himself or herself are: 'Is a team needed? Does this task require the complementary efforts of a group of people?' These raise the further questions: 'Why do teams arise in the first place? What are the kinds of task that need teamwork?'

Often the source of a team lies in one person doing a job that he or she discovers is too large for them in the time available. You can mow a large cricket field with a motor mower, but if you have an assistant to remove and empty the grassbox when full you can do the job in less time.

The examples can be developed into others where two, three, four people and so on are needed. This involves the 'author' of the group, now most probably the leader, getting to know the members, their abilities and characteristics. Initially, when they come together, he or she will be the central person, the one who will know them all individually, and they him or her, but not each other: this fact alone puts the 'leader' in the commanding position. If he or she is paying them, too, this position will be even stronger.

WORKING TOGETHER	
NATURE OF TASK	**IMPLICATIONS**
Can be carried out by a single person but time required is not available.	Several people doing the *same work* may complete the task in the given time, for example, 500 envelopes that need to be addressed, filled, stamped and despatched in the afternoon post. Each person knows what to do and does it independently.

Effort or force required cannot be exerted by one person, for example, to lift a lorry off someone who has been knocked down.	A group of people must work together. A degree of coordination will be needed between the operatives.
Several distinct operations are required at the same time or in concert, for example an orchestra.	Here someone beyond the operators may be needed to organize and coordinate, for example a conductor.

Bernard Babington Smith suggested that the kinds of task that require teamwork – a concerted effort by a number of people – can be set out as shown in the 'Working together' table above.

It is important, then, to check whether or not a particular task needs teamwork in the third sense of *complementary* effort. A class of schoolchildren working on arithmetic is a group of individuals, not a team. Of course if they tackle a history project, put on a theatrical production or play hockey they will have to work as members of a team. In the first case the working group is the *context* for individual work; in the other instances the group is an *instrument* for achievement.

In all these cases, however, the principle of cooperation or concerted effort pays off. As Homer wrote, 'Light is the task when many share the toil'. But not all match up to the following definition of a team, from M. Argyle's *The Social Psychology of Work* (Penguin):

> Teams are groups of people who co-operate to carry out a joint task. They may be assigned to different work roles, or be allowed to sort them out between themselves and change jobs when they feel like it, for example the crews of ships and aircraft, research teams, maintenance gangs and groups of miners.

EXPERTS AND TEAMS

Josephine Klein in *The Study of Groups* (Routledge and Kegan Paul), devoted her first chapter to the performance of tasks in groups. She attempted to describe more precisely in what circumstances it would be worthwhile to form a group.

Let us assume, she postulated first, that the members of a group are equal in strength and skill, and the task they perform is very simple. If some men are pulling a rope as hard as they can, the addition of another man will increase the power of the group, but it decreases the average contribution made by the members. You do not calculate the total strength of the group by adding the individual 'strengths' of members. Each man's contribution is a marginal one.

Klein cited more research studies that indicated how this kind of interaction between members may have an adverse effect on the total output of a number of persons. These disadvantages are only important, however, when the task is simple, the goal all-important to the members and the duration of the group so short that the problems of keeping members happy do not arise. Where these conditions are not present, interaction with others will support the positive aspects of the task or help to compensate for its negative deficiencies.

Klein concluded, therefore, that where the task is simple and the members equal in strength, the task will be done more effectively if there is no interaction between members, except in so far as they are organized by an 'entrepreneur' with whom they all interact and who works out the final solution.

Let us imagine, Klein suggests next, an *unequal* degree of skill among the members. Here some research studies support the conclusion that interaction between members of the group will enable the less-skilled members to solve the problems because of the help they receive from the presence of more-skilled or knowledgeable members. The expert present will develop a solution to benefit the whole group – provided of course that the problem is such that the expert solution can be recognized as correct. If it cannot be, then the group could spend a long time discussing the merits of different solutions.

The predicament of an expert in such a situation now becomes clearer. A group in such circumstances tends to distract an expert from his best performance. If he is right, but not obviously right as far as the others are concerned, he is held back while he attempts to persuade his colleagues. If he is obviously right, the group will accept his judgement but then why, you may ask, was a group needed in the first place? Most probably because the expert's decisions need to be executed by others who will feel more involved and committed if they have participated in making the decision or solving the problem. 'The expert must therefore have skill in human relations as well as in his own field if he is to function usefully in a group where other members are less skilled than he is', concluded Klein.

In addition the expert working in a group does have the benefit of testing his or her own ideas out against those of the rest of the group, a useful insurance policy against an expert pursuing a line of thought longer than is useful. For the group's comments may make him or her go back and review the problem as a whole; even the questions of untrained members may rescue an expert from following a narrow and unfruitful tramline of an approach. Here a good leader can help by facilitating suggestions and the testing of ideas between the members in group discussion. Following are some guidelines for leaders of committees or discussion groups.

CHECKLIST:
Guidelines for leaders of committees or discussion groups

- Have you understood the question, problem or need for decision, assessed the available information, and asked members to give their opinions or make their contributions?

- Do you then identify the key issues? Do you try to reach agreement where opinions differ on these issues?

- In the list of the agreed objective or policy, do you assess the value of the available contributions or proposals?

- Do you stimulate the committee to consider other options?

- Can you break down large problems into manageable pieces and deal with them systematically?

- Are you sure that the committee has genuinely weighed the pros and cons of the feasible alternatives?

- As custodian of the rules of procedure, do you interpret them firmly but flexibly?

Supposing, lastly, that a task is so complicated that more than one expert is needed to solve it. When it can be broken down into a number of smaller problems, which have to be worked out consecutively or in parallel, these smaller problems can be tackled by several experts. You need in effect a series of little experts rather than one big one in such cases. Members can make three kinds of contribution: correct suggestions, correct criticisms or 'trigger' suggestions (incorrect in themselves but triggering off correct responses in others).

Clearly we are here over the threshold of teamwork. Each member is an expert in his or her own way. Each member has a special skill to contribute to the task and can also perform some useful functions – for example, making 'trigger' suggestions – unrelated to his or her expert field.

Both Babington Smith and Klein implicitly warn us

against: (1) assuming that all tasks need teamwork – some are tackled best individually – and (2) that all work groups are teams. Committees, for example, are not the same as teams, although they are also task-oriented collections of individuals bound by a set of obvious rules.

Groups do not think or create new ideas in the way that individuals do. The individual members think and create; the group accepts, modifies or builds upon, or rejects that thinking. In that sense groups do make decisions; they may prompt and encourage but they do not create new ideas. As Tom Douglas concludes in *Basic Groupwork* (Tavistock):

> The individual tends to operate much more effectively, not exactly in isolation, but more independently in all areas of human behaviour that can be called 'creative'. No one, to the best of my knowledge, ever created anything of value as a member of a group except those factors which pertain to the group, as for instance support or reflection and exchange of ideas. Thus no painter ever created a worthwhile painting as a group. Of course there are many examples of groups executing paintings – the students of some master, like Rubens, for instance – but the guiding genius and overseeing creative intelligence was that of the master and not the pupils. Likewise no book or piece of music, no drama, no truly creative work can be performed by a group except in similar circumstances, namely, under the overall direction of a creative individual.

CHECKLIST:
Requirements for teamwork

- What are the origins and nature of the common task?

- Does the task require teamwork?

- Is it too complex for any one individual to tackle successfully on his or her own?

- In order to succeed, is it essential that there should be more than one expert or specialist in the team?

- What are the specialist skills or knowledge necessary?

- Is there a leader who can blend together expert and inexpert contributions, such as 'trigger suggestions', at every stage of the team's work?

- Is the task a creative one, best tackled by gifted individuals with assistants, together with opportunity for regular discussion with colleagues?

- Would setting up a committee, rather than establishing a team, be more appropriate?

SEQUENTIAL TEAMS

Question: When is a team not a team?
Answer: When it is apart.
Do you agree?

So far we have considered teams as face-to-face groups working together on a project. But there are many teams where members may be working out of sight or earshot from each other for much of the time. Teamwork still continues in these conditions, at least in high-performance teams.

Here work is not done obviously in concert together, like an orchestra playing a symphony. All have to work in a particular sequence: for example, the plasterer cannot do his or her work until the bricklayer has finished building the walls; the tiler cannot do his or her work until the joiner has finished the roof. How good the finished house is depends upon each doing their job properly. If only one of them does not succeed in doing this, the whole project is ruined. Remember that the major cost of the house is the cost of the labour. This is important because the final price of the house depends upon each person doing his or her work effectively and upon each person using their time efficiently.

Viewed in this sequential way almost everyone who works on their own is really part of a team. An enterprising schoolteacher used the example of the building industry to introduce a programme on teamwork in industry. The second phase was called 'Missing parts and missing people' as shown in the case study below.

Teaching teamwork in school

This report by a schoolteacher illustrates how a realistic and broad concept of teamwork can be taught in the classroom:

> In this phase we looked at jigsaws with pieces missing and saw how this can spoil the whole picture. We talked about various mechanical instruments and how they are useless if only one small part is missing or does not work. I encouraged the children to draw pictures of anything they liked, with one part missing and the others then tried to spot what was wrong with it and what effect this would have.
>
> This then led into a discussion on teams and how each member of a team depends upon each other. The children tended to think of sports teams that they are part of at school. I tried to lead them to think of other teams especially ones found in certain work situations. I invited certain people to come and talk to them about their work and their role as part of a team:

1 A postman explained the people involved in delivering any letter posted in one of our local post boxes.
2 A telephone engineer explained the people involved in installing a phone, the cables, the exchange and the maintenance of these.
3 A teacher explained how the staff of a school could be considered to be part of a team.
4 A worker in a local biscuit factory explained all the people involved in producing a packet of biscuits.

In all cases I asked the speaker to stress the importance of every person involved in 'their team' and how the final aim could not be achieved if any one member of the team was missing or did not do what was expected of them.

The way to judge the effectiveness of 'sequential teams' is to look at their performance from the standpoint of the customer or client, for this is the only person who *experiences* the result – or lack of result – of the whole team. If one member, one link in the chain, is weak that will cancel out the effects of the other members. The well-designed train may get you there safely and on time; the guard and ticket inspector may be courteous; designer, manufacturer, driver, guard and ticket inspector, as well as time-tabler, booking clerk, station manager, have all done their parts well; but if the cleaners have not bothered, and the train is filthy, the customer may well go away with that damaging image in his mind. Next time he or she may choose to travel by air or coach.

The all star team

Too many cooks spoil the broth. A chain is no stronger than its weakest link. Platitude upon platitude, but relevant.

The sequential procedure is like a multi-stage rocket where any part can fail, and the failure rate of each component determines the failure rate of the whole project.

Let us suppose we have a five-stage rocket on the launching pad. Assume 90 per cent reliability for each stage. The resultant reliability of the rocket is 90 per cent of 90 per cent of 90 per cent of 90 per cent of 90 per cent – or 59 per cent. In a five-stage rocket with 80 per cent dependability at each stage, the chance of success is only 33 per cent. Forget it.

Where successive stages in a process are interdependent, quality of performance at each phase is crucial. Putting more men on the job is not necessarily going to help – the quality has to be right. What you need is an all-star team.

Alan Simpson in *The Financial Post*, Canada

Who is leading (motivating, inspiring) in a dispersed or sequential team? The manager cannot be everywhere at the same time.

In a sense leadership has to be built into each individual member – he or she has to be a self-leader. That means not just being a self-starter in terms of motivation and work but also someone who can sustain himself or herself. He or she has also 'internalized' – both the standards of his or her profession and the team's standards. When there is no one around to chivvy, chase or cajole, these are the standards he or she will stick to.

There is an analogy here with an artist, who works alone but exemplifies one meaning of integrity: adherence to artistic standards outside himself. If the picture does not come up to scratch or the poem fails to evolve or the music is below par, the true artist throws it away. He does not need anyone else to evaluate his performance; he knows when he has done a good job.

The analogy can be taken a step further. For the author – apparently practitioner of a solitary craft – can be seen as a member of a dispersed team; some of the members – editor, indexer, book designer, picture researcher, copy editor – he or she may meet, and others – printer, salesmen, warehouse manager, bookseller – they probably never will.

Lessons from wild geese

As each bird flaps its wings, it creates 'uplift' for the bird following. By flying in a V formation, the whole flock adds 71 per cent greater flying range than if the bird flew alone.

Whenever a goose falls out of the formation, it suddenly feels the drag and resistance of trying to fly alone, and quickly gets back into formation to take advantage of the 'lifting power' of the bird immediately in front.

When the lead goose gets tired, it rotates back into the formation and another goose flies at the point position.

The geese in formation honk from behind to encourage those up front to keep up their speed.

When a goose gets sick or wounded or slows down, two geese drop out of the formation and follow it to help and protect it. They stay with it until it is able to fly again or dies. Then they launch out on their own, with another formation, or catch up with the flock.

It is quite possible, and probably very desirable, to develop in ourselves and in others this sense of being members of a team apart – or rather many teams apart. It saves the self-employed and the individual contributor in organizations from the barren rocks of individualism.

CORE PURPOSE AND AIMS

Leadership includes the notion of direction. It follows that self-leaders (members of dispersed teams) have a sense of direction. They will share a knowledge and commitment to the common task, despite being out of face-to-face interaction or even when removed from regular contact by telephone or letter. Moreover, they will have sufficient trust and confidence in their unseen leader and colleagues to know that they also are pressing ahead on agreed lines and according to accepted standards.

In this context it is not enough to know just the objectives. When people are out of contact with their manager and a problem or obstacle crops up that makes it impossible to attain objectives or compels a major deviation from the plan, what do they do?

To exercise their initiative in the proper way each member of a dispersed team must be clear about its core purpose. The core purpose is the answer to the question:

Why does the group exist at all?
or
What is the special and specific contribution it makes to some wider system (that is, the business or organization as a whole)?

This is different from defining its objectives or goals at a particular point. Of course knowledge of its core purpose is really essential for all teams. For this will serve as a navigation mark for thinking about goals, structure, priority of activities and allocation of resources. Many of the ailments in these areas can be traced back to a lack of clarity and agreement about the primary purpose of the organization.

Ideally it should be possible to describe the core purpose succinctly in one sentence. Not that any one wording should be regarded as sacrosanct; indeed that short definition of purpose should frequently be rephrased to keep it fresh and alive.

Aims are middle term – the bridges that span the river between core purpose and the more concrete, tangible, specific objectives and priorities of the next short-term. Knowing the relevant aim means that you can be flexible: if one route (objective, plan) to the goal is blocked you can still press on towards a state defined as an aim. You can take alternative routes. If you do not know the aim, the eclipse of an objective will leave you in the dark. You have no alternative but to ask or wait for new orders.

KEY POINTS: TEAMS

- A team is essentially a group with a common aim in which the technical skills and personal abilities of the members are complementary. A high-achieving team has all the properties of a more ordinary team but in an enhanced degree.
- High-performance teams tend to be the ones with clear, realistic and challenging objectives; a shared sense of purpose; and an atmosphere of openness and trust.
- They make the best use of their resources, they build on experience – including failures – and they ride out the storms.
- Each member is both an expert and skilled team member in performing functions needed by the task, maintenance and other individuals.
- Teams often grow from one person who is their author and leader; if so, such a person needs to shift the centre

from himself or herself to the cooperative efforts of the team.

- The test of a good team is whether or not its members can work as a team while they are apart, contributing to a sequence of activities rather than to a common task that requires their presence in one place and at one time.

Only he who knows his own weaknesses can endure the weaknesses of others.

Japanese proverb

9

THE LEADER

'Without a leader, wild geese do not fly very far.'
Chinese proverb

So much depends upon the quality of the leader – upon *your* leadership. This raises several questions. First, what *is* leadership? Can you become more specific about it as a prelude to devising a programme for self-improvement. Secondly, how does leadership relate to team membership? Are all members who contribute functions really leaders? And, lastly, is leadership innate or can it be developed?

To discuss teambuilding without an exploration in depth of the team leader – his or her personality and character, knowledge and experience, abilities and skills – strikes me as a pointless exercise. Orchestras may contain excellent violinists and woodwind players, there may be a marvellous composition in front of them but if the conductor is not a leader they will not produce great music. Leadership – great leadership – is the theme of this chapter.

WHAT LEADERSHIP IS, AND WHAT IT IS NOT

Many of us tend still to believe that 'a leader' implies one person dominating another or a group of people. Research studies suggest that domineering individuals are not chosen or accepted leaders by others, except in situations such as prison. Physical strength or size, a dominant personality, or a will for power over others, is not the answer.

In industry, as in every other sphere where free and able people need to cooperate, effective leadership is founded upon respect and trust, not fear and submission. Respect and trust help to inspire wholehearted commitment in a team; fear and submission merely produce compliance.

Leadership involves focusing the efforts of a group of people towards a common goal and enabling them to work together as a team. A leader should be directive in a democratic way.

For a leader is not there simply to coordinate functions. He or she helps the movement forwards in a given direction, through the efforts of individuals that complement and enhance each other. He or she recalls the group to the strengthening unity of a common purpose. A leader makes the parts whole.

Gang leader

The musical *West Side Story* is the only introduction many of us have to the world of the street gang in America. In 1927 William F. Whyte wrote a book called *Street Corner Society* about the role of the gang in the life of underprivileged boys in Boston's Italian community and in particular a gang called the Nortons led by Doc. Members formed a well understood and fairly stable hierarchy: not only did the group usually do what the leader suggested but each member's behaviour reflected his position in the power structure. Whyte decided that remarks travelled up the hierarchy during planning of group activities, and, when a decision had been reached at the top, flowed down to the lower ranks. It was not just a case of leaders telling followers what to do but a far more complex interaction between individuals in adjacent ranks. Whyte described the role of leader as follows:

> The leader spends more money on his followers than they on him. The farther down the structure one looks, the fewer are the financial relations which tend to obligate the leader to a follower ... The leader refrains from putting himself under obligations to those with low status in the group.
>
> The leader is the focal point for the organisation of this group. In his absence, the members of the gang are divided into a number of small groups. There is no common activity or general conversation. When the leader appears ... (he) becomes the central point in the discussion. A follower starts to say something, pauses when he notices that the leader is not listening, and begins again when he has the leader's attention.
>
> The leader is the man who acts when the situation requires action. He is more resourceful than his followers. Past events have shown that his ideas are right. In this sense 'right' simply means satisfactory to the members. He is the most independent in judgement ...
>
> When he gives his word to one of his boys, he keeps it. The followers look to him for advice and encouragement, and he receives more of their confidences than any other man. Consequently, he knows more about what is going on in the group than anyone else ...
>
> The leader is respected for his fair-mindedness. Whereas there may be hard feelings among some of the followers, the leader cannot bear a grudge against any man in the group. He has close friends (men who stand next to him in position), and he is indifferent to some of

the members; but if he is to retain his reputation for impartiality, he cannot allow personal animus to override his judgement . . .

The leader does not deal with his followers as an undifferentiated group . . . (He) mobilises the group by dealing first with his lieutenant . . .

The leadership is changed not through an uprising of the bottom men but by a shift in the relations between men at the top of the structure. When a gang breaks into two parts, the explanation is to be found in a conflict between the leader and one of his former lieutenants.

> William F. Whyte, *Street Corner Society*
> (University of Chicago Press, 1927)

THE FRUITS OF LEADERSHIP

One of the chief fruits of good leadership is a good team. That principle seems universal in human society, and relevant, too, to the creatures that serve man. Studies of dog teams, for example, show that Siberian huskies can reach and sustain a speed of about 20 mph provided they have a good lead dog. This is a parable, if you like, for human teams.

The characteristics of the leader and the outcomes are related. They can be tabled as shown oveleaf.

YOUR POTENTIAL FOR LEADERSHIP

Yes, there are such people as natural leaders but they are an extremely rare breed. Most leaders, and indeed some of the most successful ones, are born *and* made. By that I mean they are endowed with a naturally high potential for leadership, which they have discovered and set about consciously developing. They look upon leadership partly as an ability or skill that you can learn, practise and perfect.

Nor are leaders a 'type'. There is no one style of leadership that must be donned like a straitjacket on your personality. 'Leadership is being just *you*', said Field Marshal Lord Slim succinctly. You do not have to be an extrovert or aggressively cheerful. Successful leaders are very different. They all have

CHARACTERISTICS	OUTCOMES
• Enthuser	• People are purposefully busy and everyone has a basis on which to judge priorities.
• Lives his values, such as integrity	• Sense of excitement. People willing to take risks. People willing to take on high workloads. Sense of achievement.
• Leads by example	• Consistency. Followers know leader's values.
• Generates good leaders from his followers	• Is trusted by his or her followers.
• Aware of his or her own behaviour and of his or her environment	• People aspire to leader's example.
• Intellect to meet needs of his or her job	
• Aware of the needs of the group he or she is leading and the needs of individuals	• The led start to lead. Leader becomes less indispensable. People are delegated to, coached and supported.
• Exhibits trust in his or her followers	
• Able to represent the organization to his or her people and his or her people to the organization	• Followers feel they have some contribution to aims and are committed to them.

strengths, personality and character but these vary from individual to individual.

Consequently, an important aspect of leadership is *knowing yourself*. Knowing your own strengths and weaknesses is a key step on the path of making the most of what you have to offer. It is no good pretending to be someone you aren't: sooner or later your mask will slip. Any form of hypocrisy is anathema to a good leader. That does not mean, of course, that the leader will never act a part. He or she may have to act outwardly confident and calm, visibly stalwart and brave, when inwardly his or her feelings fall far short of these states. But here he or she is acting their best self, the person they truly are on their best days, not someone totally different from themselves.

In the context of teambuilding, knowing your own strengths and weaknesses will ensure that you compensate for what you lack. It is fatal to select people to work with you who are clones of yourself. You should deliberately choose individuals who have strengths, knowledge and experience that you do not possess in considerable measure. Humility in this sense is a leadership asset.

THE KEYS TO LEADERSHIP

'To be a leader means to have determination', wrote Lech Walesa, founder of the Polish Solidarity movement and former Polish President. 'It means to be resolute inside and outside, with ourselves and with others'.

The first responsibility of leadership is to define the objective. Achieving the aim is the ultimate test of leadership. Until you know clearly what it is you want to achieve you can't begin to direct other people towards it. When the objective or task is not easy to define the effective leader takes the time to think it out. Without a clear goal there is no such thing as concerted teamwork. Besides, who will follow a leader who does not know where he or she is going? 'If a blind man leads a blind man they will both fall into a ditch,' goes the saying.

Once the group's task is settled and the team have accepted, it is the individual's turn. He or she also needs a clear personal objective or target. Naturally it must contribute to the overall aim but the individual must see that it suits his or her strengths and skills. If possible it should be worked out with the individual concerned, so that he or she feels it their personal goal. Good targets should be:

- Measurable
- Time-bounded
- Realistic
- Challenging
- Agreed

Make sure each individual knows and feels that his or her part of the task is making a significant contribution to the group's overall task.

These elements – task, team and individual – constitute the core responsibility of the leader. They spring from the three overlapping areas of work group life already described in Chapter 6 and depicted there as 'Three areas of need' in three circles. The diagram opposite builds on this.

To fulfil the three circles of 'The leader's core responsibility' certain key functions have to be performed. They are the responsibility of the leader but that does not mean the leader will do them all himself or herself. They can be shared or delegated in all sorts of ways. The following list is by no means definitive – the sheer variety of situations prohibit that – but these general functions are commonly required:

The leader's core responsibility

Planning	Seeking all available information; defining group task, purpose or goal; making a workable plan (in right decision making framework).
Initiating	Briefing group on aims and plan; explaining *why* aim or plan is necessary; allocating tasks to group members; setting group standards.
Controlling	Maintaining group standards; influencing tempo; ensuring all actions are taken towards objectives; keeping discussion relevant; prodding group to action/decision.
Supporting	Expressing acceptance of persons and their contributions; encouraging group/individuals; disciplining group/individuals; creating team spirit; relieving tension with humour; reconciling disagreements or getting others to explore them.
Informing	Clarifying task and plan; giving new information to the group, that is, keeping them 'in the picture'; receiving information from the group; summarizing suggestions and ideas clearly.

Evaluating   Checking feasibility of an idea; testing the consequences of a proposed solution; evaluating group performance; helping the group to evaluate its own performance against standards.

It must be stressed again that not all these functions will be performed by every leader all the time. In groups of more than three or four there are too many actions required to meet the requirements of the task, team and individual for any one person to do them. But the leader is *accountable* for the three circles of core responsibility. Taken together these functions constitute his or her role. Although team members may characteristically perform one or other of them – or contribute to several – the leader makes sure that they do so. He or she may have to do each of them himself or herself as occasion requires. His or her range of functions will always be wider than any other single member.

Remember that you can be appointed a manager but you are not a leader until your appointment is ratified in the hearts and minds of those who work for you.

To deal effectively with people you must take time to understand them as persons. They need to be understood both in terms of what they share in common and what differentiates them. How does this particular person differ from all others? You do not have the *right* to know someone but you have the duty to try to do so. That does not mean being matey or familiar. It just means a willingness to spend time talking and listening. Effective leaders get about and meet people.

Give people your respect and trust, some real responsibilities together with a degree of independence and they will reward you with their best.

Lessons from history

'The best of men are but men at their best.'

Major General John Lambert, one of Cromwell's lieutenants

'I saw that he that will be loved, must love; and he that rather chooses to be more feared than loved, must expect to be hated, or loved but diminutively. And he that will have children, must be a father; and he that will be a tyrant must be content with slaves.'

Richard Baxter, English Puritan church leader on bishops who persecuted the nonconformists

'Not geniuses, but average men require profound stimulation, incentive towards creative effort, and the nurture of great hopes.'

John Collier, philosopher

'I am larger, better than I thought. I did not know I held so much.'

Walt Whitman, American poet

By contrast, if you treat people as things or numbers, they will respond without a spark of enthusiasm or an ounce of initiative. They will lack conviction and commitment. They will never discover through you that 'I am larger, better than I thought'.

Common sense should guide you in the matter of praise and criticism. Both are essential at the right time and in the right place. Judicious praise and recognition of a job well done mean a great deal to someone who takes pride in their work. It is no substitute for money or financial incentive, for praise does not fill an empty stomach. But it meets a very human need. And criticism, given firmly and tactfully in a positive, constructive way not only improves standards but also strengthens the bond of mutual respect. It shows that you care too much for the job – and ultimately for the team and the individual – to turn a blind eye to mistakes.

The proverbial wisdom of the nations has a wealth of advice – some of it contradictory – for leaders on this subject of praise and blame. Situations and the individual personalities of those concerned must guide you on which proverb to follow but the range of proverbs is thought-provoking. They reveal to us just how important giving and receiving praise is within the fabric of social life – someone once said to me that praise was the oxygen of the human spirit. But it is difficult both to give and receive it well.

Praise and blame: some proverbs

An honest man is hurt by praise unjustly bestowed
Too much praise is a burden
I praise loudly, I blame softly
Our praises are our wages
The most pleasing of all sounds – that of your own praise
Be sparing in praise and more so in blaming
Praise a fool and you water his folly
Praise is always pleasant
Praise makes good men better and bad men worse

Finally, goodness in the moral sense is the sure foundation of leadership. Honesty, integrity, moral courage, justice or fairness, all make for better, more effective teams. Virtues such as these in leader and member alike mean that the energies of the team are being spent on the task, not on infighting, politicking, back-stabbing, intriguing and mutual suspicion. As with most things, it is up to you as a leader to set the example.

KEY POINTS: THE LEADER

- The principles of leadership sound simple and obvious. Not that your job as leader will ever be simple or easy. But 'The leader's core responsibility' three circles model in this chapter will serve you as a good guide through a maze of problems and personalities towards the common goal.
- Good leadership makes everybody's work more effective and therefore more rewarding. This is *your* reward.
- You will make demands on the team and on individual members; that is what you are there for as a leader. But you should always make more demands on yourself. 'To my fellow men, a heart of love; to myself, a heart of steel,' St. Augustine said.

> *Team work is no accident, it is the by-product of good leadership.*

10

TEAMBUILDING

'To be without leaders,
to obey no one,
is unworthy of man:
it is to be like the animals.'
Vietnamese proverb

All leaders are teambuilders. For teams are always either improving or declining in effectiveness. Therefore the work of teambuilding is never done.

More specifically, teambuilding applies when you are building a team in the first place or amalgamating two teams or organizations to form a new entity, or completely reconstituting and revitalizing an old team.

Comparatively few leaders have the luxury of building their own teams in this second sense. Usually they inherit a team from someone else. The latter kind of team may include individuals who are 'brown at the edges', those who would not be there if you could start again and choose your own people. But you *can* make your own team. How do you go about it? How do you transform an assembly of individuals into a team?

That challenge may not be on your agenda now. But you

never know when you might be asked to recruit and train a team for a particular task. It is bound to happen at least once – perhaps many times – in your career as a manager. Are you ready for it?

In this chapter I assume you are the leader and can select or build your own team. But the higher up the corporate ladder you climb the more you will be involved in building teams where you are not a member. The key appointment, of course, is then the leader. It is useful to remember when making it that the team leader has very distinctive responsibilities which more-or-less define the role:

- May be responsible for selection; if not, ought to be involved in it.
- Is responsible for ensuring that the standards and discipline of the team are such that high performance through interdependence happens.
- Allocates special responsibilities and controls the use of resources.
- Directs the formation of team strategy and plans.
- Has more to do with the team's interface with other groups and individuals involved in its performance.
- Will have to make considerable demands on the team as a group and on individual members.

SELECTING THE TEAM MEMBERS

As any good cook will tell you the excellence of a meal is largely determined by the quality of the ingredients that go into it. The importance of choosing the right people as team members from the collection of possible members can hardly be over-emphasized. It is the first principle of team success.

There are degrees of choice. It is rare that a manager is

given permission – and an open chequebook – to go out into the world and choose whoever he or she pleases for their team. There are constraints on the pool of people from whom their choice must be made, as well as constraints of time under which they have to operate.

Occasionally, if there is genuinely a missing piece in the jigsaw puzzle, the leader can look beyond his part of the organization or even outside the organization itself. But compromises will almost certainly have to be accepted. You cannot be over-fastidious. Few good leaders have quite the team they would wish for, just as few good teams have quite the leader they would desire.

Shelves of books have been written on the subject of interviewing and choosing people for jobs. With the requirements of high-performance teamwork in mind, their contents can be simplified into the three key factors:

- Technical or professional competence
- Ability to work as a team member
- Desirable personal attributes

Of course it helps if you already know the people well. Sometimes the larger group from which selections or substitutions must be made is just a list of names; at other times this supply group can be a very familiar reserve – like the reserves of a professional football team – clearly involved with the current team and often considered to be not only a reservoir but also a training group – in effect, already a part of the team.

The process can be compared to a funnel; wide at the top and narrowing down to the business end. The leader or selector starts with a fairly large number of people and eliminates potential members by a process of interviewing and testing.

Technical or professional competence

What is this person going to bring to the team? The first and most pressing requirement is that he or she should possess the skill or knowledge that is needed in the team. If your team requires a marketing specialist, for example, is this person merely a capable one or is he or she likely to make an outstanding contribution in the field of marketing?

As a leader you are most probably a generalist yourself. It may therefore be difficult for you to gauge the degree of professional ability of the person before you. Arguably, if you are aspiring to lead in that field, you should have *some* knowledge for making a judgement. The modern heresy that a management science exists that can be transferred from one industry to another has bred shallow managers, those who cannot assess the competences of those who work for them. Compare that with Napoleon who once declared:

There is nothing in the military profession that I cannot do for myself. If there is no one to make gunpowder, I know how to make it; gun carriages, I know how to construct them; if it is founding a cannon, I know that. If the details in tactics must be taught, I can teach them.

Nowadays, of course, not even a military general could say the same. A leader in any field should still have sufficient knowledge to be able to assess the professional worth of the members of his or her team but may have to associate specialists with him or her to make a judgement. The conductor of a first-class orchestra will have a general knowledge of instruments. He or she may play some of them himself or herself and will be a musician, able to detect that quality in others. But when it comes to selecting a new clarinet player for the orchestra he or she may well involve other woodwind specialists, either from within the orchestra or outside it.

Given that two candidates are equal in specialist competence (and as desirable team members) preferences might well be given to the person who has a 'second string to his bow'. Many people have some other professional experience or technical expertise that is secondary to their main interest but could be highly relevant to the team in certain contingencies. You are seeking flexible people, not narrow specialists; those who can turn their minds and hands to a variety of problems with confidence.

Ability to work as a team member

In selecting dogs during trials for teams of huskies to cross Antarctica, the explorers eliminated two kinds of dog: the *non-workers* and the *disruptives*. There is a parable here for human teams. Your selection process should discover those who are not motivated – they do not *want* to achieve, they do not strive to be in the team, and they will not work hard in harness or as individuals. Like the proverbial rotten apple, such individuals will have a bad influence on the rest of the group.

Some people, however, may not appear to be well motivated, possibly because they have worked too long under uninspiring leaders in lacklustre groups. But the fire is in the flint. Consider the case study below:

John Saunders was sixty, five years away from retirement. As an academic he had produced nothing. The head of a newly-established Department of Industrial History accepted the suggestion that Saunders should join him. 'Hard luck' said his present head, 'Saunders is just a deadbeat'. Yet in the lively and enthusiastic company of six younger colleagues, all publishing books and articles, Saunders came alive. In the next ten years he wrote seven books on industrial history.

The story of Saunders illustrates how others can inspire or motivate us. Find out if the potential is there before you discard someone on the grounds of motivation.

The second sort of people to leave on one side, are those who will not make good team members because they are disruptive.

Harmony in groups is fragile enough as it is, without such liabilities as a naturally disruptive personality.

The key question to ask yourself and others relates to this factor: Is this person capable of functioning as a member of a high-performance team? If he or she is essentially a loner, or so highly individualistic that he or she cannot subordinate their ego to the common good, you will be wise to leave them to their own devices.

It is not easy or necessary to analyse too closely what constitutes this general capacity for working with others. So much depends upon the other people involved in *this* team. You have to be sensitive to the chemistry of the group.

The concept of *balance* is important here. Just as you do not want an entire orchestra composed of clarinets or flutes, so you do not want a team made up of introverts or extroverts, analysis or creative thinkers.

Once you have eliminated the non-starters you should learn as much as you can about each individual candidate. Then make your judgement in terms of the chemistry and balance of the group.

Interviews are a fairly blunt instrument for such team selection. It is infinitely preferable, if it can be arranged, to see the person in action with other members of the proposed team. If that is not possible you can possibly see them at work in another team, or at least talk to someone who has witnessed them working in groups.

For individuals soon acquire a track record among colleagues, as they do with bosses and members of their team. The best people to tell you about someone's capacity as a team member are those who have worked in harness with him or her on some other project.

Desirable personal attributes

So far you have thought about the person in terms of their technical or professional ability and their fitness for the role of team member. In both areas you are looking for a certain standard. If you have in mind the formation of an exceptional *team*, as opposed to a merely ordinary one, you will be seeking technical skills of a high order, ones that interlock with the contributions of other members of the team.

By now you will also have eliminated those with the roots of two kinds of problems in them. Those who lack the basic motivation to work hard are bound to become problems for you because their fellows in the team – intent upon high performance – will turn against them. If you select those who have a tendency to put up people's backs by their manner, conversation or behaviour, you can be sure they will cost you a great deal of time later on. Apart from the thankless task of trying to develop them – no one can turn a dandelion into a rose, however much fertilizer you use – you will expend time smoothing down the ruffled feathers of group meetings, reconciling and harmonizing like a diplomat.

Granted you are satisfied on technical grounds and you know this person is not going to behave so as to disrupt the atmosphere you are trying to build, what are the desirable extra attributes you should look for?

In a sense this whole book is designed to help you form an accurate concept of the kind of person who will work well in a team. He or she will be someone who can contribute to the *process* skills of achieving the task – especially in the areas of decision making, problem solving and creative or innovative thinking – not merely contributing from a knowledge-base to the *content* of those decisions.

Desirable attributes, if not essential ones, include the ability to listen to others and to build on their contributions. That implies a flexibility of mind. The person who is too possessive about their own 'territory' or information is setting limits to his or her own and to the group's growth as a team.

Such flexibility implies a certain lack of suspicion. The ability both to give and to inspire trust is related to integrity, which may be defined as wholeness of character and adherence to standards – professional and moral – beyond oneself. If you appoint someone to your team who lacks integrity, whatever their professional competence or superficial social 'interactive skills', you are taking a big risk.

Last on the list but still desirable come such factors as likeability or popularity of a person. Members of teams are able to suppress quite intense personal dislikes for each other over the duration of the team's working life, and being likeable to everyone is not essential. But evidence suggests that children learn better from teachers they like. On that analogy it seems fairly obvious that adults will work better with colleagues they like. Provided, of course, that personal relations do not interfere with work relations, they surely enhance all human enterprise.

CHECKLIST:
Have you selected the right team member?

	Yes	No
Task		
Has he or she an alert intelligence?	☐	☐
Where applicable, has he or she a high level of vocational skills?	☐	☐
Do his or her knowledge/skills complement those of other team members rather than duplicate them?	☐	☐
Is he or she motivated to seek excellence in results and methods of working together?	☐	☐
Does his or her track record really bear out the scores given above?	☐	☐
Team		
Will he or she work closely with others in decision making and problem solving without 'rubbing people up the wrong way'?	☐	☐
Does he or she listen?	☐	☐
Is he or she flexible enough to adopt different roles within the group?	☐	☐
Can he or she influence others – assertive rather than aggressive?	☐	☐
Will he or she contribute to group morale rather than draw cheques upon it?	☐	☐
Individual		
Has he or she a sense of humour and a degree of tolerance for others?	☐	☐
Has he or she a certain amount of will to achieve ambition, tinged with understanding that s/he cannot do it all alone?	☐	☐
Will he or she develop a feeling of responsibility for the success of the team as a whole, not simply his or her own part in it?	☐	☐
Has he or she integrity?	☐	☐
Does he or she have a realistic perception of his/her strengths and weaknesses?	☐	☐

TEAMBUILDING EXERCISES

The phrase 'teambuilding exercises' may be new but the reality is not. Its origins go back at least as far as the medieval tournaments. These provided knights with military training and the opportunity to make reputations. Individual jousting and hand-to-hand combat came first. Then there were team events. In these a group of knights fought against another group. These teams often stayed together and fought side-by-side in real battle. Team games today, such as football, baseball, cricket and hockey, are the distant descendants of such medieval tournaments.

A crucial event in the movement from being a group to becoming a team can be the teambuilding exercise. This can be based upon either (1) a substitute team task (for example, a business case study or a few days of outdoor activities) or (2) a real task (for example, going away for a weekend to plan company strategy).

There are pros and cons to both approaches. The advantage of a substitute task type of event is that success or failure is not of paramount importance. Nor are there any technological or professional challenges to meet, so that people can concentrate on the essential issue of learning how to work more effectively together as a team. The disadvantage (apart from expense) is that the activities during the event can be perceived as games with little or no relevance to the job in hand. Moreover, at a certain level of seniority, managers become less willing to learn through this medium.

The real task has the obvious advantage of reality and immediacy. But the danger is that people become so immersed in it that the training objective is lost.

How does a leader navigate his or her way through those difficulties? He or she knows that having assembled individuals into a new group, he or she has not yet acquired a team. For a team has to be grown or built through the experience of working together.

If time allows a leader can run training sessions for the group, which will have as one objective learning to work as an effective team. The tasks in these sessions may well be of the 'substitute task variety' – outdoor exercises or building towers with Lego bricks for profit. But they should never be trivial or totally irrelevant. They should also be seen as introductory to tasks which closely resemble the actual tasks that the group will be called upon to tackle together. The natural climax is the group's first real task.

REVIEWING

In teambuilding exercises careful briefing about the object is vital. Then the key part played by the *review* after the trial runs needs to be stressed. This can be unstructured. You can simply get the group together and ask 'How did the job go? Could we have worked better as a team?'

More often than not, with able managers or staff, the general discussion that follows such open-ended questions will cover all the points that the leader already has in mind. The process of reflection, digesting experience and relating it to principles has begun. The important point is to build into the programme opportunities for this unhurried reviewing or looking back on the day's work together.

A more structured approach can be followed, using questionnaires or checklists, which individuals complete and then discuss. These certainly have a place, if used appropriately, in getting a group to think critically about itself. They are especially useful if a group is unaware of the real level of its performance, or is disguising itself from some of the problems within its life it can and should be solving. The results of a checklist can then provide it with some hard evidence to chew upon.

The reviewing phase in the teambuilding activity is not temporary. A highly effective team is characterized by its tendency towards regular and searching self-evaluation of performance. Reviewing is an essential part of the process of being a high-performance team. For reviewing (and self-evaluation) to become a central feature of teamwork, certain standards have to be set and maintained. Reviewing should establish the facts first. What was our objective? Did we in fact achieve it? If we did not, in what ways did we fail?

Then you can come to *diagnosis*, introduced by the question 'Why?' '*Why* did we succeed or not succeed?' Analysis of the reasons for success or failure will start in the task circle. Was the goal clear? Did we have a workable plan? Was it communicated? Did we act flexibly, possibly altering the plan, in the face of serious difficulty? And so on.

Then you should ask questions about the teamwork circle. 'How well did we work as a team?' Here questions-and-discussion should range over coordination and cooperation, group standards (technical and social), communication, atmosphere, changes in morale, the presence or absence of mutual encouragement.

Thirdly, any deficiencies in individual skills should be explored to identify training that will remedy them. You should be careful, as a general rule, not to criticize individuals in front of the group. Remember that you are a*ppraising* performance, not acting as a negative critic, so you will point out the good as well as the not-so-good points.

Teambuilding exercises, especially if they involve one or two nights away together, provide opportunities for *developing informal relationships*. Over a drink in the bar or the meal table, team members can get to know each other better.

They can compare their different as well as similar perspectives. What are consciously and carefully listened to are the theories, attitudes, worries, values and political concerns that members of the team have about the nature, causes and consequences of the current situation. Such discussion allows members of a team to see the *complexity* of the different strands of wisdom and desires of the team and allows that complexity to be ordered or negotiated through careful discussion.

It is important for you as leader to set a high standard of listening in these informal sessions. Reflections on issues and careful exploration of individual views implies a philosophy of teamwork that is far removed from the various 'instant teamwork' recipes offered on one-day courses to managers. In many organizations people are encouraged to have as few meetings as possible and to get on with the 'real work'. But work that ignores individual values and perspectives can lead to superficial activity. In such low-performance teams, members are not committed to the activity and the quality of the team's life is not enriched by the range of experience available within it.

In conclusion, the first objective in teambuilding is to choose the right people in the light of the team's purpose. Then you should aim at developing a group identity. Giving the team a name and a base or place to meet are important steps in that direction. In the early meetings it is helpful to remember that the new members – who may know you well but not each other – are coming with the following questions in mind:

Why are we in this group?
Do we need to work as a team?
Even if it is not necessary, would it benefit us to do so?
Are we going to collaborate or compete?

Are our objectives realistic?
How are decisions to be made?
How is our performance to be appraised?
How are we going to grow in effectiveness?

KEY POINTS: TEAMBUILDING

- Teamwork is required by many tasks; even where it is not strictly needed, working as a team can transform performance and enhance job satisfaction. Good teams are not the products of chance. As a leader, one of your three major responsibilities is to build the team.
- If you are assembling a new team, concentrate on selecting individual members who will use complementary skills, techniques and knowledge and also build up the common life or *esprit de corps*. Look for those with extra qualities of personality and character mentioned above.
- Within the first year of its life, try to get your team away for a day or two on its own. With the help of a varied programme of tasks and events – practical activities followed by review – identify with team members the strengths and weaknesses of the team, listing the areas for improvement. Return home with an action plan for moving from low- to high-performance team levels.

The power of a team to accomplish its mission is directly related to how well the leader selects and develops its members.

11

CREATIVE PROBLEM SOLVING

'Three cobblers with their wits combined,
Equal Zhuge Liang the master mind.'
*Chinese saying, where Liang was a famous statesman
and strategist, first minister of the state of Shu during
the Three Kingdoms period*

By no means are all teams required to sit down as a group to make decisions, solve problems or generate new ideas. In sports teams, for example, it may be the manager and the captain who make all the decisions, while individual players solve problems posed by the opposition and play with what flair they can. In an operating theatre team, the surgeon in charge will make the key decisions; anything like creative thinking would probably be inapppropriae.

In the context of management, however, a degree of teamwork is required, both to make and implement the best decisions. This does not detract in any way from the accountability of the leader in charge. Like the surgeon, he or she must 'carry the can'. But a wise manager will involve his or her team as far as possible in the decisions that affect their common work.

The reason for this policy is not only the obvious motivational one: the more that people participate in a decision, the more they are motivated to carry it out. Each member of the team will bring a different experience, knowledge, imagination, perspective and judgement to bear upon the decision. As a result, it should be a better decision as well as a more acceptable one – providing the leader is a competent thinker himself and knows what is wanted.

To become more effective in this area, a team should have shared frameworks, drills or maps for decision making and problem solving. This chapter identifies the key ones.

WHAT IS A PROBLEM?

Many people now use the phrases 'decision making' and 'problem solving' as if they were synonyms. The processes of deciding and solving do in fact overlap but there are distinctions between them.

A decision means, literally, a cut-off point. It is the point where you cut your stream of thought about some matter. The most common reason for cutting short your mental processes is because you have made up your mind to do – or not to do – something about the matter you have been considering.

Decision implies action. After you have deliberately taken action – or no action – there will be reactions from others and from the wider environment. Some of these results you can foresee: these can be called the *manifest consequences* of your act. There are others, however, which you cannot or did not foresee – the *latent consequences*.

Let us turn to problem solving. A problem means, literally, something thrown in front of you. This can range from a puzzle to a matter that requires a decision about appropriate action. It is another very general and much-used word. At the puzzle end of the spectrum, of course, a solution does not involve action or affect your life in the way a decision might. Therefore some people – many academics, for example – can be very good at solving intricate problems like the structure of genes or the sub-atomic nature of matter and yet hopeless at decision making. Equally, good decision makers may lack some of the necessary mental qualities required in a supreme puzzle-solver.

But a problem must be problematic. If you know the answer by direct recall of facts or the application of a readily-available technique, you are not faced with a problem. (The exercise $27\sqrt{9842}$ is *not* a problem for a person with a calculator or one who knows how to perform long division.) Therefore a problem is a task for which:

- The person or group confronting it wants or needs to find a solution.
- The person or group has no readily available procedure for finding the solution.
- The person or group must make an attempt to find a solution.

This definition stresses the three essential components of a problem: (1) the motivation of the problem solvers to attain a goal; (2) the fact that the goal cannot be reached directly or immediately; and (3) the fact that a conscious effort to attain the goal is made.

The first component requires that leaders present the problems they want their teams to solve in a way sufficiently attractive for subordinates and colleagues to *want* to solve them. It is no good posing problems if the team members are not interested in attempting to solve them.

Members will probably not be able to get the solution immediately but they must feel it is within their grasp. Too often people believe that if a decision cannot be made quickly (or a problem solved speedily) it cannot be done at all. Nothing could be further from the truth!

Consequently leaders who intend to make problem solving a real part of teamwork must pay especial attention to the unique relationship that exists between task, group and individual. For they should be able to maintain morale in team and individual, in the face of repeated failures to overcome a particular obstacle, or to solve a thorny problem.

In the management context, creative thinking is best understood as one general method of problem solving. Here the novelty and unexpectedness of the course of action or solution adopted is such that we call it creativity.

To remind you of an earlier point teams, like committees – or teams in committee – are not themselves creative. It is individual members who have the bright ideas. But groups can provide a *context* in which creative thinking flourishes. Atmosphere, communication, standards, leadership, morale; all contribute to a positive climate that stimulates, triggers, encourages and develops the exploratory thinking of individuals.

WHAT MENTAL PROCESSES ARE INVOLVED IN SUCCESSFUL PROBLEM SOLVING?

Before describing a *framework* for a team to have consciously in mind when tackling problems, I want to outline the mental processes that come into play in successful problem solving.

Problem solving is integrating your previous experience and knowledge together with your natural mental skill in an attempt to resolve a situation whose outcome is not known. To make progress the group or team, like the individual problem solver, must have sufficient motivation and lack of stress or anxiety. Progress made will, in itself, fuel the fires of motivation.

The table below charting 'Some factors that influence the problem solving process' helps explain why an individual or group with all necessary knowledge to solve a problem may still fail to do so. High stress levels, lack of desire or interest and unfamiliarity with the appropriate strategies or procedures for tackling that sort of issue are some of the obstacles that can slow down progress or ultimately prevent success.

SOME FACTORS THAT INFLUENCE THE PROBLEM SOLVING PROCESS		
PERSONALITY FACTORS	**EXPERIENCE FACTORS**	**COGNITIVE FACTORS**
Stress, pressure	Age	Analytical ability
Interest, motivation	Previous professional/ technical background	Logic and reasoning
Anxiety to perform		Synthesizing ability
Resistance to premature closure	Familiarity with solution – finding strategies	Holistic
Perseverance	Familiarity with problem content and context	Valuing ability
		Intuition, flair
		Memory
		Imaginative
		Numeracy, literacy

The previous chapter, on selecting team members, covered many of the factors listed under *Personality* and *Experience* factors. Here I shall concentrate on the *Cognitive* factors – the basic mental skills given by nature, shaped by education and sharpened by training.

My argument is that we each have a profile of strengths

and weaknesses in these mental abilities. 'The Complete Thinker' – the 'Thinker for All Seasons' – would have them all in an outstanding degree, but he or she is a rare bird. Most of us are better at one or two kinds of thinking than the rest. Therefore it stands to reason that if you are building a team of ten members, and the team has applied thinking as part of its task, you do not want ten superb analysers and no synthesizers or evaluators. Otherwise you will end up with a paralysis by analysis. The principle of balance applies.

Setting aside personality and experience or knowledge considerations, what are the prime mental skills you should be seeking to include within the team? The following are the main ones:

Analysing	The capacity to take things apart, to separate out, to divide a problem into sections, to distinguish the central from the peripheral, to place things or people into categories, to dissect the complex into its constituent parts.
Reasoning	The ability (related to analytical thinking) to think in logical steps, usually from the general to the particular (deduction) or from the particular to the general (induction).
Synthesizing	The reverse process of analysing, namely the putting together of parts into a whole, assembling pieces of a jigsaw into a complete picture, placing things together so they work.
Holistic thinking	The tendency to see the whole rather than the parts, especially the way in which the whole is more than the sum of the parts. (Note that holistic thinkers tend to be hostile to over-much analysis, for the properties of the whole disappear under analysis. They are inclined to natural analogies, such as growth.) Visionaries are often holistic.

Valuing	The capacity to value accurately according to appropriate scales of worth. This is obviously conditioned by the content and context of the valuing activity, for example, valuing diamonds. But there is a more general valuing ability, for example, over people, summed up by the word *judgement*. (Note that highly evaluative people can be hypercritical of ideas, others and themselves – natural critics. The word 'critic' comes from the Greek word for a judge.)
Intuition	The faculties of analysing, synthesizing and valuing are exercised both consciously and subconsciously – in what I call the depth mind (the part of your mind that develops ideas before bringing them to the surface). Intuition is one manifestation of the depth mind at work, suggesting conclusions or ideas or ways forward without any apparent, conscious reasoning taking place. 'I have but a woman's reason – I think him so because I think him so', wrote Shakespeare. If shown consistently it is called flair.
Memory	Memory is the most important active department of the depth mind: it is our library, storage and retrieval system. There is more in it than we know, hence the ideas or thoughts of others in discussion can unlock unknown boxes in our own memories. Note that if groups or teams stay together for any length of time they also acquire something like a corporate depth mind and memory. Sometimes they need to be reminded of what they have learnt already but have temporarily forgotten.
Creativity	The ability, for example, to synthesize or relate

together two or more ideas that appear to most people to be unconnected into a new whole. Note that there is a value judgement in creativity: others have to judge the new synthesis or idea creative rather than merely novel. Closely related to creativity is imagination: the ability to think in pictures.

Numeracy/ These describe the natural abilities to think in
Literacy terms of numbers or words.

As a leader you should obviously try to sharpen your skills in these areas; they are fundamental in determining the quality of your thinking, which in turn will colour all your decisions. Elsewhere I have suggested ways of self-development in this area, for example in my companion book *Effective Decision Making*.

Think now of each member – or would-be member – of your team. What is he or she going to bring to the party? What are his or her strengths? Does he or she know his or her limitations, so that he or she is willing to listen to and accept the contributions of others? Have you any notable mental ability under-represented in the team?

A FRAMEWORK FOR PROBLEM SOLVING

In making decisions and solving problems (and I am talking here about where those two concepts overlap) it is useful to have a shared method of going about things. It may be valuable in training for the team to be taught this as a drill, as is done on many standard management courses where the drill is first explained and then applied by course members to exercises and case studies. But the best soldiers, I was once told, are those who are thoroughly disciplined and drilled in training and then allowed to revert to their natural ferocious selves!

The classic framework or general strategy for decision making/problem solving involves five steps:

ACTIVITY	NOTES
• Defining the objective or problem	Mainly analytical
• Collecting data or reviewing the information already held	Involves experience and memory as well as information-seeking or research skills, literacy (reading) and numeracy
• Generating alternative feasible solutions or courses of action	Mainly synthesizing, but the word *feasible* implies an element of rough valuing
• Choosing a right answer, or the optimum course of action	Mainly valuing, usually in decision making using more than one criterion of value
• Evaluating the decision	Either before, during or after implementing it

The drawback of this framework, useful though it is, lies in the limitations of language. We have to use words like steps, stages or phases, which imply a logical step-by-step process with each stage tidily completed before the next commences. But thinking is not neat and tidy like that, although it should always strive to be disciplined and orderly. In the actual process of thinking, the mind may dart forwards and backwards. Gathering relevant information, for example, which is nominally the second phase, will probably occur in all the other phases in some shape or form.

Understanding the Problem

- Define the problem in your own words
- Decide what you are trying to do
- Identify important facts and factors

Solving the problem

- Check all main assumptions
- Ask questions
- List main obstacles
- Work backwards
- Look for a pattern

- List all possible solutions or ways
- Decide the criteria
- Narrow down to feasible solutions
- Select optimum one
- Agree implementation programme

Evaluating the decision and implementing it

- Be sure you used all the important information
- Check your proposed decision from all angles
- Ensure that plan is realistic
- Review decision in light of experience

Problem solving guide

The nature of thinking therefore makes it exceptionally hard to lead a really effective team effort involving minds at work. Self-discipline on the part of members is essential. That will be helped if they are following a common problem solving strategy like the one above.

In the boardroom or upon many a committee much of this thinking will have been done by a sub-group or an individual commissioned to write a paper on the subject. Check that the paper obeys the ground rules that have been set for the team as a whole. Is the problem clearly stated? Is the relevant information there and is it accurately summarized? Are the feasible options set out? Do the authors make a recommendation – a tentative decision subject to approval?

Within the general framework of defining the objective or problems, generating feasible alternatives and choosing the best one, there are some more specific tactics worth bearing in mind.

The headings in the 'Guide for problem solving' table above are mainly self-explanatory. Working backwards means trying to envisage the end state and then working out what needs to be done to get there. It requires a degree of imagination. Many chief executives use this strategy now when they ask their boards, 'Where do we want to be as a company in five years time?'

BRAINSTORMING

Brainstorming is a means of generating ideas from a group of people in a short time. It works best on simple but open-ended problems where there is no one answer. For example:

> Finding a new name for a product
> Getting more people into a shop
> Getting more people to buy a product

Brainstorming is based upon the principle of deferred judgement or, as expressed by its originator Alex Osborn in *Applied Imagination* (Charles Scribner), the principle of suspended judgement. The basis is deliberate alternation of the thought process. In other words, one should turn on his or her valuing mind at one time and his or her creative mind at another, instead of trying to think both critically and imaginatively at the same time.

Yet how many of us are prepared to suspend our critical or judgemental faculty altogether, simply for fear of making fools of ourselves?

Alex Osborn goes on to give three principles that provide the foundation for group brainstorming. First, idea listing can be more productive if criticism is concurrently excluded. This principle is considered important because education and experience have trained most adults to think judicially rather than creatively. Consequently, they tend to impede their fluency of ideas by applying their critical power too soon.

Second, the more ideas the better. Those who have had the most experience with brainstorming are practically unanimous in their agreement that in idea production quantity helps breed quality. And, third, group work to produce ideas can be more productive than an individual working on his or her own. Osborn refers to numerous experiments that show how in the same length of time and under similar conditions, the average person can think up about twice as many ideas when working with a group as when working alone. These can be tabulated as in 'Four rules for group brainstorming' overleaf.

If the group falls silent during brainstorming allow silence to continue for a full two minutes before contributing. This procedure maintains time pressure as well as giving an opportunity for the individual's depth mind to work.

Following are three examples of the sort of ideas, big and small, that can come from brainstorming, or genuinely judgement-free situations.

Suspend judgement	Criticism is ruled out. Adverse judgement of ideas must be withheld until later. Do not evaluate.
Freewheel	Freewheeling is welcomed. The wilder the idea, the better; it is easier to tame down than to think up. Let your mind drift.
Strive for quantity	Quantity is wanted. The greater the number of ideas, the more the likelihood of success. Aim at, say, a hundred ideas in a period of fifteen to thirty minutes.
Combine and improve	Combination and improvement are sought. In addition to contributing ideas of their own, participants should suggest how ideas of others can be turned into better ideas; or how two or more ideas can be joined into still another idea. Hitchhike on other people's ideas.

Four rules for group brainstorming

New ways to combat vandalism on buses?

When this question was brainstormed several decades ago, ideas included personal name badges for conductors (so that they ceased to be anonymous representatives of authority), two-way radios, soothing background music, and unbreakable mirrors facing the front seats (so that people would be made aware of themselves). Today's ideas might include more single decker buses, improved CCTV, vandalism-proof surfaces made possible with new technology, or rewards for instantly reporting damage by SMS or email.

New ways of saving energy?

One 'off-the-wall' idea included a heat recovery unit that used the heat extracted from cows' milk to heat in turn the water for such processes as pipeline washing, udder washing, and calf feeding. It could reduce a dairy's electric water heating requirements by up to 60 per cent. The recovery unit was made and was found to do just that. Since this discovery, 'How to save energy?' has become a hot environmental topic and similar thinking has allowed for vital inventions that harness the energy and power of sources as obvious as the sun and wind, and as relatively obscure as the potato.

New ways of sending mail?

'... A piece of paper just large enough to bear the stamp, covered at the back with a glutinous wash, which the sender might, by applying a little moisture, attach to the back of the letter ...' An extract from the original proposal by Rowland Hill, inventor of the postage stamp. When the then Postmaster General heard of it, he exploded: 'Of all the wild and visionary schemes I have ever heard of, or read of, this is the most extravagant!

I have used brainstorming quite often on leadership training courses and during teambuilding exercises. One of the group is asked to act as a 'recorder', since it has been found that listing of ideas as they are produced gives the group access to all of its output at all times, ensuring also that no ideas are lost. The recording method that works best is large-scale (for example, using felt pens on flip chart paper or white-boards) so it is easily readable by everyone in the group. Brainstorming is most effective if the problem is simple and can be well-defined. But I have found it can contribute at all stages of more complex problem solving, from defining the problem to final details of implementation.

FOLLOW-UP

It has been demonstrated that not more than forty minutes should be allocated to the actual brainstorming session but the participants are asked to go on considering the problem and send in further suggestions. These are added to the list already obtained and all ideas are classified into logical categories by the leader. These are handed to the person who submitted the problem initially. He or she then undertakes evaluation of the list, possibly processing ideas by combination, elaboration or additions of his or her own.

Evaluation may be best done not by the brainstorming group itself but by a small group of, say, five members directly concerned with the problem. Keep the brainstorming group informed of the result otherwise they may want to be excused the next time they are asked! The steps of evaluation are:

- Decide on appropriate criteria
- Pick out instant winners
- Eliminate the useless or inappropriate
- Sort similar ideas into groups and select best of each group
- Apply criteria to instant winners and best of each group
- Submit the shortlist ideas to reverse brainstorming (that is, in how many ways can this idea fail?)

Although the main purpose of brainstorming is to generate ideas, there are many by-products that may be of considerable value. Brainstorming provides a means of finding out what people think about management problems; it helps people gain a better understanding of, and tolerance for, each other; it improves morale; it encourages initiative by making members more willing to accept and tackle problems; it increases confidence in their own abilities.

To practise your team in creative problem solving, give them some problems to solve and appoint observers who may find it useful to be armed with the following checklist:

CHECKLIST:
Team problem solving in action

- Do the group members establish a common understanding of the problem, based upon a careful diagnosis?
- Do they focus together on a single aspect of the problem, or does each member have his or her own way of seeing the problem?
- Do they actually work as a team, building on each other's ideas, or as a group of individuals?
- Do the members take pains to make sure everyone understands each idea?
- Was the technical content of the discussion at a high level?
- Does anyone use analogies to suggest possible solutions?
- Do the members really listen to one another?
- Do the members tend to shoot down ideas quickly?
- Does the group insist that each idea be a complete solution?
- Or do they support and improve on an unsatisfactory idea?
- Do they thoroughly explore one idea before going on to the next?
- Did people keep to the point and not waste time?

YOUR KEY ROLE AS LEADER

Leading a group meeting of any kind – committee or team – for the solution of a problem is a difficult job and requires both task and maintenance factors, as well as personal qualities of mind, personality and character.

Professor Norman Maier wrote an article in *Psychological Review* called 'Assets and Liabilities in Group Problem Solving' in which he made the following points:

- The skill of the leader requires his or her ability to create a climate for disagreement, which will permit innovation without risking hard feelings.
- When the discussion leader aids the consideration of several aspects of the problem solving process and delays the solution mindedness of the group solution, quality and acceptance improve.
- Problem solving activity includes searching, trying out ideas on one another, listening to understand rather than to refute, making relatively short speeches and reacting to differences in opinion as stimulating.
- For a participative group to work, the leader must concentrate on the group process, listen in order to understand rather than to appraise or refute, assume responsibility for accurate communication between members, be sensitive to unexpressed feelings, protect minority points of view, keep the discussion moving and develop skills in summarizing.

In decision making (as opposed to many forms of problem solving) a leader will have to be concerned with the acceptability of the decision to those who will be implementing it. What degree of acceptability is required? Maier's model opposite illustrates the options.

		Quality of Solution Required	
		Low	High
Degree of acceptibility required of those implementing decisions	High	Agreement needed but technical factors unimportant	Technical excellence and unanimity needed
	Low	Quick decision possible	Probable need for experts but not much discussion by others

Maier's model

Models like this are thought-provoking but they don't make decisions or solve problems. Only people meeting and agreeing upon a course of action or a solution can do that. However, too many meetings of groups and teams are badly led. For meetings are about people. Bringing intelligent and able people together inevitably means that contrasting views – if not conflicting or clashing ones – will be expressed. Your main asset as a leader is your skill in managing the resolution of different opinions and obtaining commitment to effective action.

KEY POINTS: CREATIVE PROBLEM SOLVING

- Success in problem solving requires effort directed at overcoming a surmountable obstacle. Use all available facts, inadequate as they are; seek more information if necessary as well as suggestions, clarifications and reactions. It is difficult to get away from preconceived ideas: the brainstorming technique can help.

- Disagreement can lead either to hard feelings or to innovation, depending largely upon the sense of purpose, standards and atmosphere that you as the leader create in the group. Encourage the clash of ideas; discourage the clash of personalities.
- The idea-generating process should be kept separate from the idea-evaluation process, because criticism tends to inhibit creativity.
- Seek to develop a range of feasible choices or alternatives in the middle part of the discussion, keeping an open mind for sudden or later inspiration.
- Remember that a solution propounded by you as the leader is likely to be improperly evaluated – the group tends to either accept or reject it. Make sure your ideas are submitted to the same disciplines as everyone else's.

If you are not part of the solution you are part of the problem.

12

TEAM MAINTENANCE

'I prefer association to gregariousness . . .
It is a community of purpose that constitutes society.'
Benjamin Disraeli, former UK Prime Minister

Work groups can be divided into temporary and permanent.
A temporary or *ad hoc* team or group is formed for a specific
purpose and then disbands when that is accomplished. 'Task
forces' and project groups belong to this category. A permanent or standing team continues in existence, with gaps in
membership made up by new recruits. Committees can
belong to either category.

There are pros and cons to both types of work group.
Most people respond well to having a limited commitment
of time, like a sprinter who can clearly see the finishing tape.
Against that, such groups often disband when they are just
becoming real teams in the sense defined in this book.

The chief advantage of the permanent team is that members do come to know each other and each other's capabilities exceptionally well. They should be able to work more
effectively together. But such groups can become cosy and
comfortable, like an old pair of slippers. Even assuming that
they are still fully effective, they need regular servicing and

maintenance. Then they can perform at a level of excellence over a long period. Team maintenance in that sense is the subject of this chapter. How do you keep a good team in its existing state of efficiency and effectiveness?

MAINTAINING CORE PURPOSE

It is comparatively easy to select a core purpose, recruit a team and break the purpose down into manageable aims and objectives. It is much harder to maintain the core purpose of the team, committee or group over a length of time. As a leader you should be prepared from time to time to ask yourself and the team the following questions:

- Why do we exist, what are we here for?
- What and who would be affected if we went out of existence?
- Are there more cost-effective ways our purpose and aim could be achieved than having this team?
- Has there been a significant change in our mission as a team? Have we perceived – or been given – new responsibilities?
- Are we still the right people to be tackling this work? Does it still need a team effort?

Remember that groups have a tendency to want to perpetuate themselves. The instinct for survival comes into play. We are here because we are here. Any move to disband the group can be perceived as a threat to unity. The desire for self-perpetuation *regardless of task* has taken over. The group has become a family, not a team.

Therefore as leader you must reassure yourself (if not others) at intervals that there still is a real task for this group to perform and that it still requires the degree of teamwork you are seeking to build and maintain.

MAINTAINING STANDARDS

Standards, you recall, are the group norms – usually unwritten – that largely determine corporate behaviour of the group. There may be, for example, a high standard of attentiveness to each other in one group while in another you may notice that no one is listening to their neighbour or anyone else.

Standards are technical as well as interpersonal. Ideally groups should set themselves, with some direction from their leader, standards of performance that they think they can attain. These should be neither too high nor too low but sufficiently stretching or challenging to grip interest and – when achieved – to pay a dividend in sense of achievement.

Over a period, however, two things can happen. First, the team's standards can slip. Idleness, indifference or that disease of success called complacency set in. These malaises introduce a general feeling of 'anything goes here'.

Secondly, the world outside the organization changes. Standards in our given field or industry are constantly rising. What seemed to be high performance, high productivity or good sense to the customer ten years ago, now seems mediocre judged from an impartial standpoint.

One first-aid remedy for declining standards is to generate a sense of competition. The fat and lazy manager entered for a marathon has some incentive to become lean and active. So it is with groups and organization. The first step is for you, as leader, to bring home to the team that, good though its performance is, it is no longer good enough. 'Good enough for what?' ask the anxious team members. 'Good enough to beat the competition', you reply.

Competition, you recall, deals with relative positions on a league table. But the true end of competing with others is not the transitory pleasures of winning. The true end of striving against competitors is to raise your standards against some absolute scale of value. That goal is summed up by the word *excellence*. To compete means literally to seek something together. Actual competitions should be regarded as incentives, milestones, even games but not the real object of the exercise.

It is not much good holding up absolute values like 'excellence' to a team with slipping standards. Your words will sound abstract and banal. But tell the team or organization where it stands in relation to the competition as factually as possible. Invite them to tell you why they are so low on the scale. Formulate with them some plans that will take you further up the ladder within a given time.

COPING WITH CONFLICT

What do you do if the team threatens to fall apart because there is personal conflict between two or more members? By conflict here I mean primarily a clash of personalities rather than ideas.

The first strategy is to attempt to depersonalize the issue so that the difference of ideas or policies becomes central. This is not easy because personalities and issues tend to become intertwined.

As a prelude to discussing conflict in this wider sense it may be useful to chart the ways the different individuals are responding to the fact of conflict of ideas between them. Do they adopt one of the following behaviours outlined in the table opposite?

Competition/Forcing Tries to force his or her own way/ideas through.	Gets result; all right when quick concerted action is required. If idea/course of action is bad, time is wasted; teamwork reduced; other views not heard.
Collaboration/Confronting Brings issues into the open in order to explore all feasible options. He or she will move all the way if convinced.	Quality of results is better; commitment of team is higher. May take a long time, and is frustrating for people looking for early decision.
Sharing/Compromise He or she is willing to negotiate a halfway position, and is therefore prepared to move that far.	Everyone gets something; no one solution is preferred. May be only way to get a result. But the quality of the compromise solution or decision may be inferior and commitment to it poor.
Avoiding He or she opts out when conflict arises, waiting for others to solve it; avoids taking up a position.	Reduces tension. May result in good ideas being lost. Usually leads to a shelving or postponement of the conflict, not its resolution.
Accommodation/Smoothing He or she is worried about hurting other people's feelings by seeming to disagree with them. Leans over backwards to avoid giving offence or to repair 'the damage'.	On unimportant issues may be best way of maintaining group unity. Can seem patronizing. Poor solutions often go through because of lack of challenge.

Pros and cons of different responses to conflict

It can help individuals to see that they have fallen into one mode of handling conflicts of ideas and that there are other options open. It is good sometimes to experiment with a bolder style if you happen to be timid by nature, or a more compromising, open and accommodating approach if your natural tendency is to try to dominate 'the opposition' with your own ideas.

Returning to interpersonal or intergroup tension: it is a matter of judgement to decide at what point the tensions begin to turn into conflicts that will seriously impair the work of that team and which call for intervention. But you must, as a leader, be ready to make that judgement and then take appropriate action.

Should you decide that confronting conflict will lead to higher cohesiveness eventually, the next step to realize is that you do not hold all the cards – only half of them. If there is a conflict between A and B in your team it is going to be primarily those two people who resolve it – or it will simply fester and splutter on. You can help in various ways as mediator. You can bring some pressure on them: the various non-violent forms of 'knocking their heads together'. For example, you can set a time limit in which you want their differences to have been settled, suggesting a third party arbitrator to help. Or you can offer to act in the role of consultant, catalyst or change agent yourself to bring about reconciliation, although it may be difficult to combine that role with being leader and therefore ultimately accountable for the work of the team.

Attention to the feelings or emotions of people in conflict situations pays dividends. But whether or not to encourage people to express their negative emotions towards each other, privately or in public, must always be a matter of judgement, for there is a calculated risk to be taken either way. Will it lead to improved relationships, or is the cure worse than the illness? A close scrutiny of the situation and personalities will usually tell you the right answer.

The ultimate resolution of conflict usually stems from the emotional discovery – or rediscovery – that we need each other if we are going to complete the common task. If both individuals or parties value that common task, albeit for different reasons, they will be willing to make the necessary sacrifices and adjustments. The advantages of cooperating to achieve results prove stronger than the displeasures of inter-necine warfare. If reasoning fails and the conflict worsens, you may have to make radical changes in the composition of the team.

To return to an earlier theme, you should help team members to distinguish between the ideas of a person and the person himself or herself. Getting team members to see the good in each other – and to accept it while living with their private or open rejection of other parts of their colleague's personality – is part of the teaching function of leadership. It is an aspect of personal development, of growing together in maturity.

The ideal, of course, is to have a high level of mutual trust, respect and – if possible – affection between members of the team combined with a toughness towards each other's ideas. What should be central is the common quest for the truth of the matter. In that pursuit the blows may come thick and fast but they are not perceived or taken as being personal in any way, just as two professional boxers trade punches. Each member of the team has learnt how to accept the other person while rejecting his or her idea if it merits rejection.

THE CASE OF THE POOR PERFORMER

Dr Neutrino is a lecturer in the Department of Astronumeric Engineering. He has been in the University since his late twenties and is now fifty-three years old. He has done little or no research, except for two short papers ten years ago. His lecture course produces poor examination results. Final year degree students have commented that his notes and example sheets are insufficiently rigorous. His teaching style is barely adequate. His colleagues find Neutrino has become apathetic; he is unenterprising and unwilling to exert himself. He does not initiate any exchanges with the students but is helpful when approached. He is frequently absent or late arriving. Despite all this he is likeable. His colleagues have been tolerant about his shortcomings for several years but now the necessity for improving standards of the department is very real. For Astronumeric Engineering will suffer from the cutbacks in government funding and some departments – the less good ones – will have to close in two years time; no one knows which ones. The last head of department had some rows with Neutrino but then gave up – partly because Neutrino hurt *his* feelings by what he said about the department and partly because he did not like rows. 'The University cannot sack Neutrino because he has security of job tenure', he explained to you when you took over as departmental head six months ago. But Neutrino's colleagues are getting more restive; three of them have been to talk to you about him privately in the last month. As leader of the team what are you going to go?

There is no short and simple answer to the case of the underachieving member in your team. The strategy for finding an answer, however, is plain.

First, you must *diagnose* the causes of underachievement.

It may be lack of motivation, inadequate training and poor leadership in the past. It may be that the person is in the wrong job – Neutrino should never have been a university lecturer. Still, as a leader you are like a golfer who has to play the ball where it lies.

If possible, check out your interpretation with the person concerned. He or she may add to, or subtract from, that picture of cause-and-effect you are trying to construct. Do not treat the symptoms, address the causes.

Ask Dr Neutrino what *he* wants – what motivates him now. He may want early retirement; if so you will be more than willing to help him achieve it. He may want to become a full member of the team but in a different role: perhaps more in an administrative capacity. List the *feasible options* for him and with him. But 'carrying on as we are now' is not allowed on the list!

An underachieving member may dispute the fact that he or she is so. Be prepared to tell him the impression created by his behaviour in the department; what is observable to you and others – with some concrete examples in reserve to produce if necessary. This may lead into a discussion of Neutrino's attitudes. But you should avoid delving into his personality – positions central to the person – for that cannot be changed.

The end result should be an agreed action plan to restore the individual as a fully effective member of a team that is setting its sights and standards higher today than yesterday. That plan, like all plans, should be flexible. There should be a 'contract' with the person concerned to review progress at agreed intervals. The contingency option of parting company must always remain if that progress is not forthcoming.

CHECKLIST:
Does your team need maintenance?

Does your team need maintenance? The following questions will help you to decide:

- Are there any symptoms of low morale, such as a decline in the team's self-confidence, a weakening of resolve and a loss of a sense of purpose?

- Has the group or organization lost its sense of direction?

- Is each individual member still clear about the team's core mission and its principal aims? Are personal goals or objectives related to that purpose?

- Is the atmosphere of the group negative and lukewarm?

- Are individual members lacklustre in their enthusiasm?

- Has communication between members been dwindling?

- Are there signs of mistrust developing?

- All groups have potential 'metal fatigue' cracks. Are those cracks widening into divisions between individuals, cliques, or sub-groups?

- Have professional and personal standards declined in the last six months?

- Can you identify one or more individuals who are clearly underachieving when measured against today's group standards?

- Are there complaints about your leadership?

If you have answered *yes* to seven or more of these questions you need to maintain or build the team anew. Go back to the beginning of this chapter and reread it carefully until an action plan begins to take shape in your mind.

KEY POINTS: TEAM MAINTENANCE

- Teams, like friendships, need to be kept in good repair. Their purpose should be kept bright and burnished; their standards should be rising incrementally and their cooperation becoming ever closer and more effective.
- You should encourage the clash of ideas, not personalities. There is enough conflict outside the organization without fighting each other. Remember the African proverb: 'When the elephants fight it is the grass that gets trampled'.
- Being on the same side should help you to develop hard debate in your group without the side effects of emotional hurt and interpersonal bitterness.
- Never rest content with your team's level of performance: if they are *that* good they can be better tomorrow. Team maintenance is about removing those obstacles that prevent you growing as a team.

Do not be so busy on the common task that you forget the common life.

13

A CHECKLIST FOR TEAM LEADERS

In this last chapter I want to instil the desire to become more effective in the role of team leader. For the more skilled you become as a leader, the more rewarding you will find it to be. *Enjoyment increases and the burden lightens.*

There are a growing number of courses on leadership skills, both public ones and 'in-company' ones, in larger organizations at any rate. These can help you to develop your own leadership and team membership skills, especially if you attend them at the right time in your career: just before or shortly after taking up a leadership role.

But others cannot really teach you leadership – you must learn it yourself. Establish your own strengths and weaknesses as a leader with ruthless objectivity. Then set to work over a reasonable time span. Remember that any self-development worthy of the name takes a considerable stretch of time, so start young if you can. Just as no man is born wise or learned so none is born a leader. Confidence is a plant of slow growth.

The following checklist is designed to help you apply the principles of this book to your team now. Doing things differently, making improvements there, can be the first steps on your much longer road of self-development as a leader. 'An inch is a cinch, a yard is hard', as one modern proverb goes.

Do not be afraid of making mistakes on that journey. Failures teach success. They also teach humility.

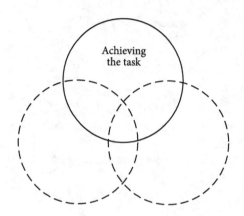

TASK

		Yes	No
Purpose:	Am I clear what the task is?	☐	☐
Responsibilities:	Am I clear what mine are?	☐	☐
Objectives:	Have I agreed these with my superior, the person accountable for the group?	☐	☐
Programme:	Have I worked one out to reach objectives?	☐	☐
Working conditions:	Are these right for the job?	☐	☐
Resources:	Are these adequate (authority, money, materials)?	☐	☐
Targets:	Has each member clearly defined and agreed them?	☐	☐
Authority:	Is the line of authority clear (accountability chart)?	☐	☐
Training:	Are there any gaps in the specialist skills or abilities of individuals in the group required for the task?	☐	☐
Priorities:	Have I planned the time?	☐	☐
Progress:	Do I check this regularly and evaluate?	☐	☐
Supervision:	In case of my absence who covers for me?	☐	☐
Example:	Do I set standards by my behaviour?	☐	☐

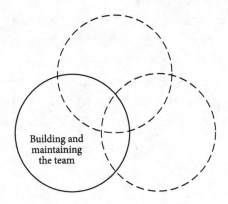

TEAM MEMBERS

		Yes	No
Objectives:	Does the team clearly understand and accept them?	☐	☐
Standards:	Do they know what standards of performance are expected?	☐	☐
Safety standards:	Do they know consequences of infringement?	☐	☐
Size of team:	Is the size correct?	☐	☐
Team members:	Are the right people working together? Is there a need for sub-groups to be constituted?	☐	☐
Team spirit:	Do I look for opportunities for building teamwork into jobs? Do methods of pay and bonus help to develop team spirit?	☐	☐
Discipline:	Are the rules seen to be reasonable? Am I fair and impartial in enforcing them?	☐	☐
Grievances:	Are grievances dealt with promptly? Do I take action on matters likely to disrupt the group?	☐	☐
Consultation:	Is this genuine? Do I encourage and welcome ideas and suggestions?	☐	☐
Briefing:	Is this regular? Does it cover current plans, progress and future developments?	☐	☐
Represent:	Am I prepared to represent the feelings of the group when required?	☐	☐
Support:	Do I visit people at their work when the team is apart? Do I then represent to the individual the whole team in my manner and encouragement?	☐	☐

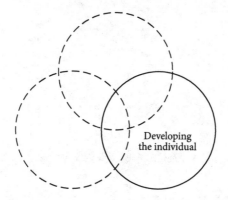

INDIVIDUAL

		Yes	No
Targets:	Have they been agreed and quantified?	☐	☐
Induction:	Does he or she really know the other team members and the organization?	☐	☐
Achievement:	Does he or she know how his or her work contributes to the overall result?	☐	☐
Responsibilities:	Has he or she got a clear and accurate job description? Can I delegate more to him or her?	☐	☐
Authority:	Does he or she have sufficient authority for his or her task?	☐	☐
Training:	Has adequate provision been made for training or retraining both technical and as team member?	☐	☐
Recognition:	Do I emphasize people's successes? In failure is criticism constructive?	☐	☐
Growth:	Does he or she see the chance of development? Does he or she see some pattern of career?	☐	☐
Performance:	Is this regularly reviewed?	☐	☐
Reward:	Are work, capacity and pay in balance?	☐	☐
The task:	Is he or she in the right job? Has he or she the necessary resources?	☐	☐
The person:	Do I know this person well? What makes him or her different from others?	☐	☐
Time/attention:	Do I spend enough with individuals listening, developing and counselling?	☐	☐
Grievances:	Are these dealt with promptly?	☐	☐
Security:	Does he or she know about pensions, redundancy and so on?	☐	☐
Appraisal:	Is the overall performance of each individual regularly reviewed in face-to-face discussion?	☐	☐

CONCLUSION
EFFECTIVE TEAMBUILDING

'In our complex and interdependent
world, vulnerable to disruption, few things
are more important than the quality
and credibility of leaders.'

Anon

I have emphasized the role of the leader in teambuilding. It is essential for organizations to develop individuals who are skilled at building and maintaining teams. I have assumed that you are such a leader – potential or actual. Lastly, I have suggested that, if you are trained to lead, it will help you be more effective when you are working in the role of a team member. For most managers wear at least two hats: leader and team member. The ideal is to reach excellence in both roles.

In temporary or *ad hoc* groups an important part of your role as leader will be to manage the interface between the team and its sponsors and clients, transmitting their message to the team. It is a two-way traffic: you also need to secure the necessary outside resources for the team. Directing (setting aims and objectives), facilitating the interdependent contributions of members as a team, relating to each individual member in a positive constructive way; these are the essentials of the role of leader.

Example is all-important in teambuilding. It is not an easy path. Most of us can echo Shakespeare's words in *The Merchant of Venice*:

> I can easier teach twenty what were good to be done, than
> to be one of the twenty to follow my own teaching.

As a leader you have to embody truth, not theorize about it. The role of team member is positive. Its very lack of structure invites you to be creative in it: more like playing jazz music extempore than following a composer's score.

Active attentiveness, building on ideas, testing ideas with criticism, making suggestions; all these are manifestations of someone who sees team membership in this positive and constructive light. In other situations you may be the appointed or elected leader but here you have 'contracted' to serve as a team member. This means you will behave in a certain way. You will make your view known but will loyally accept the 'lawful authority' of the leader and actively support him or her. You can, for example, complement him or her by supplying missing functions in the task, team or individual areas. For the perfect leader does not exist. Your leader will have weaknesses. See them as opportunities for helping, not occasions for carping to colleagues. Good team members can make poor leaders look good and better leaders look excellent. It is a creative role in that sense as well.

Individualists, as opposed to individual persons, will find these skills much harder to acquire and practise. Having a strong preference for doing things your way makes it difficult to work within the constraints of a team effort. Of course it depends upon how strong your bias towards individualism proves to be. Not all individualists are loners. Individual specialists of outstanding ability may often be difficult to work with but it is a price both leader and the rest of the team are prepared to pay in return for their gifts. The challenge is to create an atmosphere in which those gifts can flourish, and also where they can learn to cooperate with others and produce their best. In time the 'prima donna' may come to see that he or she is powerless without the 'full supporting cast' of the team, and modesty – living within one's true limits – may begin to dawn.

We often picture a team as a number of people running around on a playing field, working together in one place or sitting around a table making decisions.

Yet teamwork is equally important when the team is physically dispersed. Much of the work of teams or organizations is done by individuals working on their own.

Such team members need vision or imagination if they are to work as a team even when they are apart. They need to see the whole, for instance the end product as experienced by the customer or client. For the latter are often receiving pieces of teamwork in a serial fashion. First, metaphorically, the electricians wire up the room and then the plasterers arrive. It soon becomes apparent *to the customer* whether the building firm (or its equivalent) is working as an effective team or as merely a collection of individuals fulfilling roles, individuals or groups out of touch – often out of sympathy – with each other or with other groups in the same organization.

The complexities of modern organizations, especially those that operate consciously or unconsciously on the matrix principle, lead inevitably to role conflicts. The electrician may want to wire your house but he or she belongs also to another team working on the brewery down the road and is wanted there. Who has the prior claim on his or her services? Who decides?

Teams need to develop common standards that they will adhere to while working apart. These will be in addition to the professional, technical or craftsmanship standards inculcated by vocational training. They include standards about communication with each other as well as the team spirit of service to the customer. Creating this climate or atmosphere, establishing common ways of doing things, this is your responsibility as leader, although you would be wise to enlist all the help you can get. Let your influence travel with each team member.

If you are a competent leader and a person of professional and personal integrity, a leader who has won the respect of those that work for him or her and beside him or her, people will say this about you. He or she:

- Is 'human' and treats us as human beings
- Has no favourites; doesn't bear grudges
- Is easy to talk to – listens and you can tell
- Keeps his or her word and is honest
- Doesn't dodge unpleasant issues
- Always explains why – or else why not
- Is fair with praise as well as criticisms and criticizes without making an enemy of you
- Is fair to us as well as the company
- Drives himself or herself hard so you don't mind him or her expecting the best of you

You will be getting the required results, your group will be working purposefully as a team, and each individual feels he or she is playing a vital part in the success of the group. The ultimate 'Three circles of great teambuilding' then begin to take shape:

Three circles of great teambuilding

INDEX

Page references in **Bold** denote complete chapters